D0150447

PRAISE FOR

CHRISTIAN CHINA
AND THE LIGHT OF THE WORLD

For more than four decades, David Wang has been a pioneer in telling the world the inspiring yet sobering story of the Church in China. In his latest book, *Christian China and the Light of the World*, he focuses on the lives of the leaders of China's fast-growing urban churches. We come to know doctors, entrepreneurs, surgeons and sales executives who have given up lives of prominence and prosperity to follow Christ as pastors, evangelists and even missionaries abroad. Through his detailed, personal narratives of the lives of Chinese who we only know by their Christian names, Wang offers insights into the challenges and struggles of China's urban Christians and suggests lessons that their experiences may provide for the worldwide body of Christ. This book is both informative and brilliantly relevant.

David Aikman
Author of *Jesus in Beijing* and former *TIME* magazine correspondent

When you talk with David Wang about the urban church in China, as I have many times, you cannot help but be infected with his enthusiasm for this new expression of Christ's Body in China. I know of no greater apostle and mentor to China's urban church than David. He has challenged urban church leaders to work hand in hand with China's government to address the needs of Chinese society, and through his efforts a much higher level of training in pastoral leadership has been made available. As you read this book you will experience a firsthand report of what God is doing in this new day of openness in the People's Republic of China. If you are wanting to understand how modern missions can best impact the future of China's church, you need to read this book.

Jon Davis
Lead Pastor, Beijing International Christian Fellowship

We live in an exciting new season. The center of gravity of world Christianity, which began in Jerusalem and through the centuries reached North America, has now shifted to the Asian Pacific Rim. China is the dominant nation there and China is destined to assume leadership for the Christian movement for the foreseeable future. My friend David Wang's title reflects what I have just said: *Christian China*. This is a book that will enlighten your mind and warm your heart. As you read it, you will fall in love with China and you will begin to move into God's new stream for the future.

C. Peter Wagner
Vice-President, Global Spheres, Inc.

One of the amazing happenings in the world's history of church growth has to be the so-called "Third Church" in China! Encouraged by the modernization movement in the 1970s and 1980s, huge numbers of rural youth have rushed into the cities for education, jobs and a new life. This avalanche of young and eager hearts gathered in a new environment has created tremendous yearning and spiritual hunger—hence the marvelous growth of the urban church in China. A veteran missionary and researcher of church growth, Dr. David Wang has served us with another well-written book in *Christian China and the Light of the World*. His succinct descriptions provide us with inspiring pictures of the joy, glory, pain and grief among the urban church members in China. It is indeed a book to be read by anyone who is interested in China, her church and her people!

Rev. Thomas Wang
Former General Secretary, Chinese Coordination, Centre of World Evangelism
Founder, Great Commission Center International

大大荣耀！

Christian CH基督教NA

AND THE LIGHT OF THE WORLD

MIRACULOUS STORIES FROM CHINA'S GREAT AWAKENING

David Wang with Georgina Sam
COAUTHORS OF *STILL RED*

Regal

For more information and
special offers from Regal Books, email us at
subscribe@regalbooks.com

Published by Regal
From Gospel Light
Ventura, California, U.S.A.
www.regalbooks.com
Printed in the U.S.A.

All Scripture quotations, unless otherwise indicated, are taken from the *Holy Bible, New Living Translation*, copyright © 1996, 2004, 2007 by Tyndale House Foundation. Used by permission of Tyndale House Publishers, Inc., Carol Stream, Illinois 60188. All rights reserved.

Other version used is
NIV—Scripture taken from the *Holy Bible, New International Version®*. Copyright © 1973, 1978, 1984 by International Bible Society. Used by permission of Zondervan Publishing House. All rights reserved.

© 2013 David Wang with Georgina Sam
All rights reserved.

Library of Congress Cataloging-in-Publication Data
Wang, David, 1946-
Christian China and the light of the world : miraculous stories from China's great awakening /
David Wang, Georgina Sam.
pages cm
Summary: "China...a Christian movement numbering in the tens of millions. The rapidly expanding economic power of the most populous nation on earth puts China front and center in any discussion about the future of the globe. But is there more to China's story than money? Christians in North America have many questions about the People's Republic of China and what is rumored to be a Christian movement numbering in the tens of millions. Christian China is the essential guidebook for North American Christians to understand and pray for their sisters and brothers in China's cities. Readers will find not only facts and data, but also true accounts of Chinese believers' great exploits as they follow the Holy Spirit into the future."
—Provided by publisher.
Includes bibliographical references.

ISBN 978-0-8307-6732-8 (pbk.)

1. Christianity—China. 2. China—Church history—20th century.
3. China—Church history—21st century. I. Title.
BR1288.W35 2013
2013022725

Rights for publishing this book outside the U.S.A. or in non-English languages are administered by Gospel Light Worldwide, an international not-for-profit ministry. For additional information, please visit www.glww.org, email info@glww.org, or write to Gospel Light Worldwide, 1957 Eastman Avenue, Ventura, CA 93003, U.S.A.

To order copies of this book and other Regal products in bulk quantities, please contact us at 1-800-446-7735.

This work is dedicated to the memory of Wang Mingdao and Allen Yuan Xiangchen. It is also dedicated to Samuel Lamb and Miao Zhitong, both of whom passed away as this book was going to print. They are the original inspirations and trailblazers for the urban house churches in China.

Contents

Foreword

BY DAVID AIKMAN

I first came across David Wang four decades ago not long after I had arrived as a reporter for *TIME* Magazine in Hong Kong. I was a young foreign correspondent and this was my first assignment overseas. The bailiwick or "beat" of the handful of reporters based in the Hong Kong Bureau was to cover South-East Asia, China and Taiwan. I had been sent to the bureau because I had studied China and Chinese in graduate school and knew more about the country than many reporters covering the country. What most of my superiors at *TIME* hadn't known was that I was a committed Christian. In addition to wanting to understand political, economic and social issues in China, I was fascinated by China's religious scene.

Of course, to most observers of China, there was no religious scene at the time. China was still in the throes of the disastrous and cruel Great Proletarian Cultural Revolution, a political movement initiated by Mao Zedong in 1966 that had torn like a tornado through China's religious landscape. Temples, mosques, churches and cathedrals were closed down throughout the country and sometimes were pillaged or destroyed altogether. Christians had been arrested, publicly humiliated, sentenced to long prison terms and sometimes executed. Ownership of a Bible could get you thrown in prison, or sometimes persecuted to death by Mao's Red Guards. The general consensus of China-watchers was that the Christian faith had seemingly vanished from China as completely as if it had never existed. Jiang Qing, Mao's wife, had even told foreigners visiting China in 1975 that Christianity in China belonged only in a museum.

How wrong she was. But I would not have known this unless I had made the acquaintance, and then gained the friendship, of David Wang, then the director of the Hong Kong office of Asian Outreach. Associates of Wang, and other Chinese from Hong Kong with whom he had talked, had stories of mini-revivals starting up in towns like Fuzhou, on the coast of Fujian province. Then refugees from China who trickled out of China to Hong Kong by swimming the dangerous, shark-infested waters separating Hong Kong's islands from the Mainland, began to speak to reporters about interesting religious developments in southern China. In one instance, I was able to "triangulate" Asian Outreach's stories of revivals by interviewing a Public Security official who had defected from Fuzhou. He had been tasked with cracking down on the revival, but had been converted to Christ after witnessing the character of the Christians he had observed.

Later I was based in Beijing but quite regularly visited Hong Kong and received informative briefings from David Wang. Later still, I was based in the United States and came through Hong Kong several times in my pursuit of the story of the Chinese church. I was always struck by how well David was connected in China, not just with Christian leaders in the house churches and the government-connected Three Self Patriotic Movement, but with high level municipal and provincial officials. I eagerly sought out David whenever I had an opportunity in Hong Kong.

David has written previous books about China. But in *Christian China and the Light of the World*, he goes far beyond the retelling of China's remarkable Christian growth story. He examines the ways in which China's Christians have learned to cope with the challenges to their faith brought by modernity and capitalist prosperity, with all of their temptations. Moreover, China's Christians have remained aware that they constitute an important—perhaps a decisive—component of the transmission of the gospel to every corner of the world.

Not only should students of the gospel in China pay attention to the lessons in this book, but also students of the global spread of the gospel in any and every country. This is not a fantasy narrative like *Jurassic Park,* but an equally riveting glimpse into the Christian future—not just in China, but perhaps worldwide.

David Aikman
Former *TIME* magazine correspondent in China
Author of *Jesus in Bejing: How Christianity Is Transforming China and Changing the Global Balance Of Power*

Principal Characters

Job, orthopedic surgeon and pastor, Wuhan

Abraham, pastor, Shanghai

Ruth, businesswoman and pastor, Wuhan

Paul, pastor, Xiamen

Caleb, entrepreneur and pastor, Chengdu

Daniel, businessman and pastor, Wenzhou

Benjamin, church worker, Shanghai

Note: These individuals introduce themselves with English names when they speak with foreigners.

Prologue

*You are the light of the world—
like a city on a hilltop that cannot be hidden.*

MATTHEW 5:14

HE KNEW HE WAS BEING WATCHED. His choices had been made perfectly clear to him: "If you go to Shanghai, you'll be arrested. If Abraham comes to see you here, the two of you will not be allowed to meet."

"But we just want to pray together." Job recalled how he had tried to reason with the men in the black coats.

"No way," the men in black replied. "Praying together is a meeting. You're planning to rebel against the government and we won't allow it."

Job contemplated his options. He wanted to be a friend—a brother—to do his part to support Abraham, but he didn't want to antagonize the situation unnecessarily. It was tense enough already, with unregistered churches in the major cities of Beijing and Shanghai being shut down for the first time since Deng Xiaoping's reformation of the nation in the late 1970s.

Thankfully, the crackdown hadn't reached his city—at least, not yet—and the local authorities needn't have warned him about what would happen if he went to Shanghai. He knew, too, that they were just trying to do their job when they told him that a meeting couldn't happen in their jurisdiction either.

But this wasn't making the decision any easier. And if he thought his own situation was difficult, how much harder must Abraham's be? Somehow, the authorities were aware of every single step Abraham took. He couldn't visit anyone without being asked about it. The police even followed his wife and children when they went to work and school. His emails were being monitored, as were his phone calls. He had tried changing his mobile phone, but within several hours they had called him on the new number to let him know they knew. When he'd checked into a hotel so they wouldn't bother him (or his family) at home, they had knocked on the door in the middle of the night. Using a fake name to try to get a little bit of quiet time didn't work either. They had still managed to find him. Talk about feeling suffocated.

基督教

Job and Abraham were really feeling the pressure in 2009. In fact, the trials and difficulties experienced by Abraham's church, Wan-bang, or All Nations Missions Church, were even reported by the international media. News services such as the Associated Press, and well-established mainstream daily papers like the *Wall Street Journal*, the *Guardian* in the UK and the *Australian* ran stories that commonly cited the Wanbang Church in Shanghai, among others, as one of the Chinese government's current targets, whose activities were being restricted. Wanbang Church had even received mentions in the China sections of the United Nations Refugee Agency's (UNHCR) *2009 Report on International Religious Freedom,* and the US Department of State's *International Religious Freedom Report 2009*.

On the surface, these stories of churches being shut down and Christians detained, interrogated and harassed in the Mainland were not unusual. After all, this was China, and as the believers there say, "These things happen here. The work of the Lord continues regardless." Yet, the case of Wanbang Church (and Shouwang Church, or The Watchtower, the church from Beijing that was regularly named in tandem as another example) was different. The two were anomalies among house churches in the People's Republic of China (PRC).

Both Wanbang and Shouwang did not behave in the way house churches normally did when the government came to put pressure on them. They didn't run away. They didn't scatter. They didn't hide. Instead, they made a stand. After they were locked out of their regular church premises, the members boldly kept on gathering to worship God, even choosing to meet outside in freezing, snowy conditions.

The actions of the two largest house churches in the country's leading cultural and political cities ultimately proved to be the line in the sand, distinguishing the urban house church as unique from the rural house church.

基督教

In Shanghai it all began a year earlier. Occasionally, the officials would simply attend a church service at Wanbang. Sometimes Abraham would be invited out for a "cup of tea" with them—which, in the Mainland, was parlance for an official rebuke—although these meetings would tend to be in the form of a polite conversation. Specifically, the officials would talk to Abraham about the "influence" of his church.

In a few short years, this body of believers had grown from some 300 people to 1,500. Who could tell where the growth would stop? They could see it for themselves. The people were enthusiastic; they were excited and energetic. They were motivated—and the goal was emblazoned in a clever slogan on a banner spanning the dais in the sanctuary: The church was aiming to raise and train 333,000 cell group leaders.

"Wouldn't it be better if you were part of the Three Self Patriotic Movement?" the officials asked Abraham. "Join the official church, and together we can all influence so many more people in the city—and you wouldn't have to change anything that you're doing now. We could be one church, two systems."

The suggestion was evocative of the late Deng Xiaoping's proposal in the early 1980s for reunification of the country with Taiwan, Hong Kong and Macau. But Taiwan never agreed with the principle. Abraham felt he couldn't either. The church isn't a political institution. It didn't seem right to apply a political solution to a matter of faith.

Halfway through the year things began to turn uglier. There were clear, deliberate attempts to intimidate the members of the church. Having accessed the church's database through an informant, the authorities implemented a systematic plan to harass and coerce people into leaving or quitting the assembly, beginning first with the newcomers and progressively moving on to the more longstanding members before targeting the leaders and staff. The officials also began visiting Abraham at least once a month. By the end of August, the police raided the church premises and confiscated computers, CDs and other files.

In November, it was official: The Wanbang Church was banned. A chain and police tape sealed off the entrance to the premises as if it were a crime scene, and no one was allowed to cross the line for the purposes of worship. The landlord could enter the premises, though; the government told him that he was free to find a new tenant and rent the space out again.

For a while, the church in Shanghai held their meetings outside in a parking lot. But pressure was brought to bear on the remaining members. They could feel the noose tightening when a ring of police surrounded them at their meetings, and they were subjected to one-on-one questioning. "How long have you been attending this church?" they were asked. "Do you have to give money to the church? What does the pastor teach? Does he ever say the government is not good? What is your job? Where are you employed? Where do you live? How old are you?" Not surprisingly, some could not endure the constant pressure and left. Abraham grieved for every member lost.

Feelings of betrayal were hard to overcome. There were other house churches in the city—fellowships that he and his church's ministry team had gone to in recent years, at the churches' request, to provide leadership training. Why did they not stand up with his church now? Even friends from the assembly had left—including fellow pastors. He could not have imagined that.

During that time, advice seemed to flow freely from anywhere and everywhere. Suggestions came to him from inside and outside of the country via text messages, phone calls, emails and face-to-face conversations. "Stop what you're doing. Spare the flock. Get away from there and hide yourself." This was the kind of warning counsel that would usually come from the believers in the house churches.

On the other hand, some foreigners just couldn't understand why the church would not register with the government. "Is it really such a terrible thing?" they would ask. "Wouldn't it save everyone a lot of trouble, especially you and your family, if you just signed up? How could you allow your family to go through all that?"

There were so many different opinions, so many varying voices, given with different motivations despite good intentions—and these were only from the Christians! How could one know what was the right step to take? Amid the conflicting voices and the turmoil, Abraham came to realize that there was no true unity among Christians, even among the house churches in China. How could there be when everyone was speaking something so different from what others were saying? While he appreciated that people were sincere in their sharing, and in their personal convictions, still it was conflicting counsel.

How could people expect him to run away? Abraham wondered. *How could others expect him to register?* Of course he shouldn't give in to pressure, but he certainly wouldn't run. He considered the history of the rural underground Church. Throughout the years, from what he could see, the believers saw their assemblies go through waves of rapid or explosive growth followed by official crackdowns, which led to a period of some subsidence and the need to keep as low a profile as possible (or hide altogether), only to be succeeded by another round of substantial growth. The cycle seemed to be un-necessary—build up, tear down, hide; build up, tear down, run away. When would it ever end? Surely it wasn't right that this course go on and on. He came to a decision. His mind was now made up. He would not perpetuate the cycle. He would make a stand.

基督教

The decision to stand in the face of an official shutdown in China is atypical among house churches. The much more common response is to react like a fugitive—to escape, to get away from the place. That, at least, has been the way Christians from the rural areas have traditionally dealt with persecution and pressure in the Mainland. It's a survival tactic that has been employed and honed by necessity through the years. But who could argue with it? It was, after all, initially in the countryside, in the simple home gatherings, that the Church in China first experienced revival and booming growth under Communist rule. Though vigorous efforts were made to eradicate Christianity in the years up to and including the infamous Cultural Revolution, the Chinese Church flourishes today primarily because of the seeds of faith, perseverance and longsuffering planted by those rural believers.

Since the founding of the People's Republic of China (PRC) in 1949, there have been two main streams feeding the nation's growth of Protestant Christianity. The institution of an atheistic regime ended up creating a spiritual vacuum, which in turn led to a personal awareness of the emptiness within. This realization came in large part to the people in the countryside first, sparking the rise of the first stream, the aforementioned house church. (Yet it should be noted that "atheism" does not necessarily equate with one having "no religion" or "no faith." As some of the Christian leaders in the Mainland say, there is no such thing as *absolute* atheism, because the atheist's belief will be placed in money, knowledge, science, technology or something else.)

The second stream is, of course, the government-approved Three Self Patriotic Movement church (TSPM). However, it is the unsanctioned house church—specifically the rural house church—that in the darkest moments was the main catalyst driving the Church's extraordinary growth.

Until recent years, the rural underground Church formed the majority of the estimated tens of millions of Christians believed to be living in the Mainland. (Some unofficial figures today actually reach upwards of 100 million.) Moreover, many of the amazing stories of miraculous healings and other signs and wonders originated in the countryside.

With the advent of Deng Xiaoping's Open Door Policy in 1978, spiritual renewal also began to come to the cities. The urban house churches, fledgling at this stage, were not as plentiful or far-reaching as those in the rural areas; but the gatherings did, for the most part, consistently resemble those in the countryside, as it was not uncommon to see the gifts of the Holy Spirit in operation, including the manifestation of miracles and other signs and wonders.

Overall, the effect of the Open Door Policy was such that many Chinese citizens, for the first time in their lives, gained exposure to things beyond their borders—through studying or conducting business abroad, interacting with foreigners visiting the country and, more recently, accessing diverse domestic and international sources of information through the Internet and other media. The emergence of consumerism, materialism and large-scale urban development eventually became more widespread, beginning in the eastern coastal provinces and gradually moving westwards inland to the central regions. Suddenly, Chinese citizens, particularly in the cities, found more choices and options open to them than ever before.

Nineteen eighty-nine proved to be a watershed year. The Tiananmen Square crackdown shattered illusions and severely shook belief in the virtues of the Communist Party. It spurred people, particularly the intelligentsia, artists and journalists, and even some of the Party's old faithful, to question the meaning of life. These groups of people lived primarily in the cities and were the main beneficiaries of the country's economic growth, which had been on a steady upward trajectory for a little more than a decade at this point. They had been able to garner a taste of personal choice and prosperity, similar to citizens of industrialized nations, yet this horrendous tragedy had occurred. Their newfound riches had not been able to prevent something like this from happening. What good, then, were the changes in their society?

Tiananmen Square became a turning point for China. It was the cause of the Communist Party's crisis of confidence.

To this day the effects of that crisis continue to linger. Without Tiananmen Square there would not have been the widespread urban soul-searching, the personal reflections or questions about the value of pursuing money, wealth and material goods. Without Tiananmen Square there would not have been the revival of faith and religion in the cities. A new third stream would not have arisen to feed the growth of Christianity in China.

This was the point in time when people, particularly those in the cities, began to literally flock into churches in their desperation to fill the emptiness within and find truth. They did not require any formal presentation of the gospel—or informal, for that matter. They did not even feel the need to ask who Jesus or God is. Ready and open, they simply asked, "How can I become a believer?"

Furthermore, with the government more concerned with maintaining security and stability in the aftermath of the crackdown, which then led to the persecution of some Christians, this newly restrictive atmosphere only further fueled the growth of the urban Church. In the eyes of those searching for truth, the official attempts to invalidate the Christian faith served to legitimize it all the more. If the government is opposed to it, so the reasoning went, it actually must be good for us. Without Tiananmen Square, there would not have been an urban house church movement.

基督教

The urban church is distinct from the rural house church. While it has experienced significant growth and dynamism in recent years, not unlike its rural counterpart, the urban church, or "Third Church," as it is sometimes called, is a separate entity in its own right.

The composition of the urban church, to begin with, is different. Urban believers have come to know Jesus through a variety of ways: Some have heard the gospel while they were overseas;

others have learned of the good news from foreigners in China; and still others initially attended the government-approved TSPM churches and then, for various reasons, came out to join the unregistered urban assemblies. Some pastors of the urban church have even received training and accreditation from TSPM seminaries. This connection with the TSPM is notable because, whether by divine plan or not, it markedly positions the urban church to be a natural bridge between the other two streams of Protestant Christians in the country, which are historically mistrustful of each other.

Members of the urban house church are more likely to come from the middle class, to be wealthier, more highly educated and tech savvy in comparison with their rural brothers and sisters. The core of the urban church leadership is derived primarily from the post-Cultural Revolution generation of converts and, in the view of the older generation of Christian leaders, have yet to truly *chi ku*, as the Chinese would say, or "eat bitterness"—that is, to endure suffering or hardship. Rather, they have grown up in a time of increasing prosperity and wealth, of ever greater opportunities, choices and, some would even say, freedom.

In some ways, life in the developing country has shifted so quickly and dramatically from "famine" to "feast" that it has further accentuated the spiritual vacuum inside people, and even the government has become concerned about the inner well-being and overall morality of its citizens. In recent years, for example, the authorities, ever apprehensive about the spread of vices throughout the country, have felt the need to clamp down on nightclubs connected with the sex industry in major cities, including Beijing, Guangzhou and Nanjing.[1] They have also issued new broadcasting rules for reality, talk and dating TV shows,[2] which were prompted by the vulgarity and questionable values that popular programs like *If You Are the One*, in Jiangsu province, were promoting.[3] The new rules, announced in late 2011, also called for provincial television news stations to include programming for shows about morality and ethics.

There has been official focus on young people—concern that they are not always able to grow and develop into proper citizens, and that their areas of vulnerability, apparently, can include direct foreign influences. Hence the dictate issued to universities to be more hands-on and proactive in influencing the inner lives of their students, which the *Washington Post* wrote about in a report published in December 2012.[4]

The leaked internal Communist Party document, which was written by a branch of the Central Committee, and disseminated in 2011, stated, "the college years are a critical time in the establishment of a person's world view, view of life and system of values." For that reason it was important for the higher education institutions to help them "resist" the foreign influences and follow the party's "suggestions," one of which was to "expand mental health education and psychological counseling" for the students. By offering such services, so the rationale goes, the students would have less reason to fill the void within with religion, particularly Christianity, which is easily accessible through the large number of foreign teachers and exchange students readily found on many Chinese campuses these days.

Other ideas were mentioned, as well, such as, to "conduct extensive heart to heart talks" with the students, "answer difficult questions," "dispel confusion" and "guide their emotions." To further combat the foreign influences on their campuses, it was also recommended that "during religious holidays"—i.e., Christmas and Easter—the tertiary schools should "make targeted living, study and sports and recreation arrangements for students."

During this time, society in the Mainland has grown accustomed to a Big Brother that is less intrusive in the personal lives of its citizens. For Christians, this has meant that some of their churches are moving premises—from what were originally less formal house gatherings to more structured meetings in commercial buildings, like offices or retail spaces. This is especially the case with those fellowships that have seen significant growth, such as Abraham's church. (Out of habit, the assembly may still be referred to as a "house" church, though some choose to classify themselves as an "unregistered" church, to further distinguish themselves from the TSPM.)

The base of the urban church is thus invariably unique from that of the rural house church, whose founding members had to literally survive such cataclysmic Maoist initiatives as the Anti-Rightist Movement, the Great Leap Forward and the Cultural Revolution, and whose conversions were a result of witnessing or personally experiencing miracles, often in dire circumstances.

The generation gap also shows in the way the believers handle persecution, at least for the time being, with diverging responses to pressure. With the fugitive mindset generally found in the rural house church during times of pressure, the advice Abraham often received from his countryside brothers and sisters was understandable. It would appear, however, that the urban church—at least in Beijing and Shanghai—is choosing to stay and face their accusers. The jury is still out, and the Shanghai church may have felt differently, but in Beijing, when the Shouwang Church was locked out of its regular meeting place, the result was an expression of greater unity among the capital city's house churches. Many other fellowships chose to join the Shouwang assembly's worship in Haidian Park in late 2009, despite the snow and sub-zero temperatures.

Perhaps because of their higher education and more extensive travel experiences, the urban church has been quick to embrace modernization, innovative ideas and technology. It has also easily integrated and utilized them in adroit ways to benefit their church growth. The unity expressed in the park for the Beijing church could not have happened without the relaying of messages through cell phones and computers, just as the rest of the world would not have been able to watch what happened there in near-real time without YouTube, at least until the video fell victim to the censors. Until the mid-1990s, stories of explosive church growth in the rural areas of China only trickled through to the rest of the world via word of mouth and conventionally mailed missionary newsletters, which would often arrive weeks or sometimes months after the fact.

The urban church also makes more deliberate efforts to evangelize the lost in a tangibly organized way. While a member of the rural house church would not hesitate to share his or her faith with someone in need, this is generally done on an informal one-on-one basis. The urban church, however, is adding another dimension to its witness by strategically planning to reach out to the community as a whole through social development programs and compassion ministries. In some areas it has even forged ties with the local government to help build up the community in practical, as well as spiritual, ways.

The urban church is purposeful in its visibility, and its efforts are arguably being noticed. A skeptic might say that it *should* be more visible given its physical location, yet even the *China Daily* has observed that the city house churches are "thriving" and that members of the TSPM churches, which are also located in cities (and primarily in cities), are choosing to move to unregistered urban house churches.[5] If the government-approved national newspaper is reporting about this trend, this suggests that there must be a different quality about the urban church. There must be more to the phenomena of the urban church than meets the eye.

基督教

Exactly who or what characterizes the urban church in China? How successful will they be in their endeavors? What will their emergence ultimately mean for the Church in China as a whole? Will they prove to have an influence on the wider global Church? If so, in what way?

The answers to these questions take on even more significance when one considers the fact that for the first time in the nation's history, more people are living in metropolitan regions than in the countryside. At the end of 2011, according to figures from the National Bureau of Statistics of China (NBS), 690.79

million people were residing in the urban areas, as compared with 656.56 million in the rural.[6] In other words, the number of people living in China's cities and towns today is more than twice that of the entire population of the United States!

And what of the rural house church? What will become of it? Given the shift in population and changes to lifestyles, what kind of impact can the believers who reside there continue to make on the Church in China as a whole? Once the trailblazer paving the way forward, do the rural brothers and sisters acquiesce meekly and diminish quietly, or do they adapt to the ever-evolving society around them to further fuel the spiritual development and maturation of the urban church?

Overall, there were 252.78 million migrant workers in the country in 2011, according to the NBS.[7] Where did these migrant workers go? The majority headed for the urban centers. Nearly two-thirds of them (63 percent), or 158.63 million, were employed in jobs that were *away* from their home province.[8] Most young people today who originate from the rural areas know that their best hope for earning a living and, generally, for improving their future financial prospects lie in working in the cities. It's the new normal in their day and age: They need to be willing to move away from their villages, at least for a while.

Among the internal migrants are the rural Christians who have decided to relocate to live among the masses, which are less to be found out in the sorghum and rice paddy fields and more in the concrete jungles. These are the offspring of an older generation of Christians who went through the refining fires of persecution, who were publicly denounced and shamed, imprisoned in labor camps and tortured, even unto death. They carry the same fire of passion in their hearts as their parents to fulfill the calling in their lives to serve their Lord Jesus Christ, to preach to the lost and to serve the needy. But, recognizing that China is undergoing transformation, they have changed their tactics and embarked on a new journey to plant house churches in what is unfamiliar territory for them—namely, the urban areas.

What is more, many of their own children envision following in their footsteps to go and make disciples. The advantage that this younger (third) generation has over their parents and grandparents is that they have been quicker to adapt to the modernization of the country and, in particular, to life in the cities, having moved there earlier for work or school.

Where will all this lead? This book, *Christian China and the Light of the World,* is but the first chapter of answers to these questions. It is an introduction to a few of the urban church leaders and the critical issues they face on the frontlines in the cities as the race to win and build up this nation's new Christians has only begun.

Just as this younger breed of believers has undergone a paradigm shift—not just in adapting to literally a new physical world around them, but also in redefining their *raison d'être* as individuals—so too must believers the world over. Thirty years ago, the West was still caught up in the Cold War; today it grapples with a surge in Islam and the challenge that more extremist elements represent to its liberal civilization. Meanwhile, people of faith in the PRC continue the (often delicate) balancing act of adhering to their beliefs and their pursuit of holiness while living to face another day without fear of official reprisal, and also trying to keep pace with the rapid modernization of society.

It is the perennial battle: right versus wrong; light versus darkness; freedom of choice or not—all packaged in the styles, colors and trimmings of the twenty-first century. Our responses should not necessarily be the same as they were in the twentieth century. There are many lessons to be learned and insights to be gained from the new generation of Christians in China. He who has ears, let him hear (see Matthew 11:15).

Notes

1. Song Shengxia and Fu Wen, "Major Cities Crack Down on Sex Trade," *Global Times,* June 8, 2010.
2. Lin Yunshi, "New Broadcast Rules Take the Color Out of TV," *Caixin Online,* October 26, 2011. http://english.caixin.com/2011-10-26/100317870.html.
3. Justin Bergman, "China's TV Dating Shows: For Love or Money?" *TIME,* June 30, 2010.
4. William Wan, "Chinese Leaders Still Suspicious of Religion, Party Document Shows," *The Washington Post,* December 18, 2012.
5. Wu Yiyao and Cui Xiaohua, "House Churches Thrive in Beijing," *China Daily,* March 17, 2010.
6. An, "China's Urban Population Outnumbers Rural for First Time," *Xinhua,* January 17, 2012.
7. National Bureau of Statistics of China, "Statistical Communiqué of the People's Republic of China on the National Economic and Social Development," February 22, 2012.
8. Ibid.

1

The Colonel's Daughter

Wherever you go, I will go; wherever you live, I will live. Your people will be my people, and your God will be my God.

RUTH 1:16

"CROSS-CULTURAL MISSIONS—THAT IS MY LONG-TERM VISION," said Ruth. "I'm constantly seeking God's will about this, trying to mature my understanding of what our role is in the big picture. How can we better prepare ourselves for the missions ahead?" When speaking of *our* and *we*, the senior colonel's daughter was referring to the wider Church in China, as well as herself.

"God doesn't just have an eternal plan of salvation," she continued. "He also has a big plan concerning how the gospel will be spread and how nations have a part to play in this. Consider the Back to Jerusalem movement,"[1] she cited as an example. "Consider the fact that it involves countries along the ancient Silk Road and winds up in Israel, a civilization that has existed for thousands of years. Our country, our culture has survived for just as long, and I believe that God already ordained and chose to prepare China for this time."

A taller and larger woman, in the northern Chinese vein, with a short bob haircut, Ruth went on to share her conviction that God's choice of missions destinations for the Church in China is strategic, as is the timing of the nation's rise to prominence on the world stage. She noted that in history the Muslim conquests were able to spread beyond Persia (modern-day Iran) and Central Asia, into the northern parts of the Indian subcontinent, and deep into Europe. In the East though, the Muslim armies were stopped at the borders of China. They were not able to actually penetrate into the

Middle Kingdom. "China," she concluded, "was the strong force in the East then, and it still has that role to play in the twenty-first century. Today, however, the point is not to 'stop' Muslims. It is to reach them with the love of Jesus Christ."

基督教

The first seed for cross-cultural missions, most believers in the house church will acknowledge, was planted by the Protestant missionaries who originally came to China in the early nineteenth century. Overseas missions began to take on greater importance in the British and American churches as a result of the Great Awakening in the English-speaking world; and in 1807, Robert Morrison became the first Protestant missionary to serve in the Mainland. After more than a quarter of a century of dedicated ministry in China, Morrison left behind a Chinese translation of the Bible, a Chinese dictionary for Westerners and a handful of Chinese converts.

The indigenous movement for Chinese cross-cultural missions first began in the early 1940s. The burden on the hearts of the native missionary pioneers was to plant the cross of Jesus in every Muslim and ethnic minority community along the historic silk trading routes. Inspired by the words of their Lord in Matthew 24:14, that the "Good News about the Kingdom will be preached throughout the whole world" before "the end will come," and by the Western missionaries who had traveled to their country, forerunners such as Mark Ma, Mecca Chao and Grace Ho formed gospel bands to preach and traverse as many of these routes as possible.

While the gospel bands did succeed in planting several churches, they were never able to move beyond Xinjiang province and Tibet. The new Communist government closed the country's doors in 1949, and the first missionaries from the Mainland would live out the rest of their days in their northwest China mission fields.

Since the PRC began opening up in the early 1980s, however, it has been the goal of the house church to pick up the baton from that earlier generation of missionaries. In 2007, the bicentennial of Robert Morrison's arrival in China, the house church declared its intention to begin repaying what they call the "gospel debt" by sending out missionaries of their own.

"The Chinese Church received a gift from the Western missionaries," says Ruth. "It's now time for us to pass on the gift. It's now time for us to preach and serve other peoples, just like they did."

基督教

Ruth is clearly a capable woman. The daughter of a war veteran from both the Sino-Japanese and Korean Wars, and a Chinese herbal pharmacist, she is a person accustomed to seeing things go her way. She is not easily moved once she has made a decision, yet she is humble and knows that to which she has been called.

"I'm a businesswoman," she says with matter-of-factness. "That's who I am. God is not calling me to be a bishop or a great preacher. He's not calling me to be famous. I'm an ordinary person called to disciple others."

Ruth may not be a celebrity, but she is most definitely a pastor. She has been leading her church in Wuhan for more than eight years. Wuhan, the capital of Hubei province, is considered the political, economic, financial and cultural center of central China. With a population of more than 10 million people, according to the nation's 2011 census figures, it is also the largest city in central China.

"There is real value in something as simple as loving the people around you," Ruth continued. "For me, that means being a good mother, a good daughter and a good boss. The most important thing is to follow God's heart, not pay attention to what others think of me."

Ruth is a picture of calm, assurance and tranquility as she speaks. She is a woman who knows her God, loves Him and trusts Him implicitly.

"The moment I prayed the sinner's prayer," said Ruth, remembering when she first came to the knowledge of His saving grace, "I could feel that *that*—Jesus—was exactly what I needed in my life. I felt like I had finally found the reason why I was living. The reason I exist in this world became so clear."

After that, she said, everything just fell into place. Ruth went on to explain how she had no mentor or older sibling in the faith to teach her what to do next. She instinctively began her own regimen of daily Bible reading, praying and singing praises to God.

Every week she would also attend the Sunday service at a Three Self Patriotic Movement church, regularly inviting different friends and clients to come along with her. Her friends were open to the invitation to attend church because they saw big changes in Ruth. The once devout Buddhist had become a committed Christian. The obstinate woman was now more patient and loving. Serious intensity had given way to transcendent peace.

Eventually, they began asking her for advice about life and spiritual matters. Before long, a small discussion group emerged around her and met together regularly. The discussion group evolved into a fellowship that soon after decided to leave the Three Self church and form its own house church. There was no particular reason for leaving the Three Self, says Ruth, except that she felt a responsibility to personally look after the people who were gathering around her. She had noticed that other people had left the Three Self church to form their own house groups to care for believers, so she figured she could do the same. The house church was formed in 2004, and Ruth, in addition to caring for her family and running her own company, managed to squeeze in time for further education. She eventually picked up enough Bible courses and credits along the way to become an ordained pastor in 2010.

The church, at almost a couple hundred members consisting chiefly of professionals, businesspeople and other white-collar workers, is not large, but it has been growing slowly and surely. Many of the members are experienced in the marketplace and have seen success in their practices and businesses, she says. But when it comes to their walk with the Lord, they are "very child-like" and they "put a lot of their trust in the Word of God and are faithful in their prayer life."

There have been times, though, when the church has had to intercede for some of the businesspeople. "We've had to pray quite often for God's intervention in their businesses when they've encountered problems," she said frankly. On those occasions the investment decisions were not necessarily wise.

More often, the hardest prayer battles she has encountered in the church have been for families—for the healing and restoration of broken marriages, and for the children. In modern China, marriages are facing an onslaught, with divorce no longer a rarity. Adulterous affairs are explosive charges that can severely test spousal relationships. Not surprisingly, Ruth feels an affinity for the wives in her church who have fallen victim to their husband's infidelity. She herself experienced something similar, so she has been able to keenly identify with these women.

The battle for the children and youth, meanwhile, is for their souls. If they are not struggling with angst about their mothers and fathers, they are being inundated with all things carnal—sex, drugs, alcohol, rock music culture, celebrities and pop stars. The environment they are being raised in is totally unlike that of earlier generations in the country, and parents today are in need of real wisdom to know how to deal with their kids' rebellion against traditional values. "This is another area that we need to stand in the gap for," Ruth said.

She said with a laugh, "God knows me really well. He knows I can easily become proud, so He would not allow me to have a mega-church. The important thing for me is to daily live out the truth. It wasn't my preaching that brought the people together—I know this well. It was because people could see how my life changed when I found Jesus."

基督教

Before she found Jesus, Ruth went through a dark time. It began when she made the horrifying discovery that her husband was having an affair. Never one to shy away from confrontation, she took him to task for it. Tempers flared, and they fought: He was a liar; she was pigheaded. He couldn't be trusted; she was controlling and only cared about making money. Back and forth the accusations flew, and each new charge was like a dagger stabbing deeper into her heart. How much suffering could one take? This was no way to live. It wasn't good for her, and it wasn't good for him. And it certainly wasn't good for their son. Divorce was the only option.

If dealing with the insult, injury and shame were not enough, Ruth then found that her once successful auto repair business was reeling from the effects of her protracted personal problems and was barely managing to stay afloat. In all honesty, she didn't know how long her business would be viable.

She also started drinking, and every extra cup of rice wine she downed brought on agonizing bouts of self-loathing. She knew that her recently acquired habit made her less disciplined, more inclined to slothfulness and prone to anger and impatience. She was not at all pleased at what she was becoming.

She felt she should be better than this. She was a senior colonel's daughter who had enjoyed all the perks and benefits of a privileged upbringing. She was a university graduate whose career had had an ideal start. Her path had been lit up as clearly as the runways her father had serviced in the People's Liberation Army Air Force: The first job she was ever assigned to was in a factory that assembled the PLA's fleet of planes. In a short time, she was promoted to the procurement department, which accelerated and expanded her learning about airplane and automobile parts.

After a while, she figured out how the different components went together, and this knowledge eventually made it possible for her to open up her own car repair shop. She had even enjoyed a small notoriety; it was a novelty for customers to find a female mechanic in the local market. But now it was all falling apart. How had she ended up here?

The only glimmer of light she found at this time was the fact that she had obtained custody of her son. He was her hope and comfort. He was her joy. He was all she had to live for.

As a mother, however, she was soon laden with a new worry. She lived with a constant fear for her boy. He was only 13 years old; how would he cope with all the changes? Would he become embittered and angry? (Having tasted enough of this herself in recent days, she did not wish this for him.) Would he become rebellious? It would be hard enough to enter the teen years, but now he would also have to learn to live with the reality of no longer having a father around. Would he grow up to be all right?

Ruth had never really known what betrayal or hardship was until her husband's affair had been exposed. Its uncovering was like the toppling of the first block triggering a domino effect in her life. One by one, piece by piece, different areas began to fall. As the situation in her home nosedived, so too did the revenues at her shop. Then the never-ending worry about her son began to weigh on her mind day and night. How she longed for the mundane stability of the factory days—at least she was assured of a regular paycheck so that she could feed and clothe her boy. That would have been one less thing to worry about.

A vicious cycle of negative thoughts began to torment her, as did a sense of desperation that seemed to be growing by the day. If something bad should ever happen to her son, she would never forgive herself.

Another feeling emerged: If the opportunity arose, she should take all the help she could get, for his sake. So she decided to act on a friend's suggestion to go to the temple and make an offering of incense. She reasoned that she had to at least try.

Though it wasn't the norm when she was growing up (there had certainly been no temple in her childhood neighborhood—an exclusive residential compound for high-ranking officers of the PLA), it seemed as if everybody was doing this nowadays. The traditional Buddhist and folk religions no longer carried the stigmas they used to, and even appeared to be enjoying a revival. In fact, the officially atheist country she was born and raised in would actually go on to become the host of the first ever World Buddhist Forum in 2006. Who would have thought that would ever happen? It was as if society had become religious overnight.

Some of Ruth's friends went to the temple to ensure that the gods would favor their businesses and allow them to get rich. Still others went to alleviate the guilt of their consciences when they accepted bribes or cheated in other ways. There were also people who went to ask for a miracle solution to a problem, such as having the means to get married, to repay gambling debts or to be healed from an illness.

Ruth, however, just wanted to keep her requests to heaven simple. In front of the incense cauldron, with her joss sticks in hand, this mother asked for only one thing: that her son would not become rebellious. *He is actually a good boy,* she thought to herself. She just didn't want him to change. But there was never any telling what effect divorce and puberty would have on a child.

She began to go to the temple at least twice a month. For extra insurance she also erected shrines in her house and at her shop. There was a shrine in her living room. There was a shrine in her kitchen. There were shrines in the hallway, in her shop's reception area, in her office—in short, anywhere there was room. Over time, nothing drastic seemed to change in her son. Her shop went bankrupt, but he remained a good boy. And the latter was all that mattered.

基督教

Her worries, however, still persisted. The questions in her mind never ceased. Were her offerings of incense on behalf of her son accepted by Buddha? What would happen to her son if she stopped making offerings? Had she set up enough shrines? Should she put up more? How could one secure the favor of her god?

She tossed the questions out to her friends in an attempt to find some answers. On the one hand, the Buddhists encouraged her to just keep burning the incense—it would be the only way to keep heaven appeased and thus ensure the welfare of her son.

On the other hand, she discovered there were some who said Buddha was not the way to heaven. Instead, this group, including Job, said that heaven could only be achieved through believing in Jesus Christ, God's one and only Son. This reply intrigued her and prompted a whole new set of questions from her. What qualified Jesus as the only way to heaven? Did this mean He is better or more powerful than Buddha? With so many gods out there, how could one actually know which one is the true God? What is truth, anyway? There were many conversations about the Christian faith between Ruth and her friends who believed in Jesus.

Ruth had to admit that she could see there was a difference in Christians in the marketplace. Usually, their behavior was not like that of the typical worker. There was honor about them—an integrity in their dealings. They also seemed to her to be somehow more civilized and polite, cultured even. And Ruth knew that these friends who were encouraging her to believe in Jesus were generally not the type of people to jump on just any bandwagon. She knew that Job, for instance, was a man of science; he was practical and not whimsical or impulsive. Yet, he had converted to Christianity.

More importantly to her, though—and this was one thing that she could clearly see—they all had a peace that she didn't have. She thought about her anger and the drinking that had developed since her divorce. Both were becoming more of a habit than she would like to admit. She thought about all the shrines she had set up and all the incense she had burned. They were the antithesis of all that she was trying to achieve and be as a person. They were supposed to give her peace of mind, relieve her troubles, provide some comfort, but they didn't. She was just more uptight.

Her friends were saying that Jesus was the only way to heaven and there was nothing anyone could do to earn His love. Even more, they said, Jesus was not just a go-to God when you have a problem in life that needs solving. He *is* life, they said. He came that each person might have life—not just her son, but her too—and that they might have it to the full.

Based on her friends' testimonies, Ruth decided that she would try Christianity. She wanted the peace and true acceptance—and they seemed to have it. She had neither with Buddha or the traditional gods. Subsequently, she committed her life to Christ in 2003.

Upon becoming a believer she was overwhelmed by the love of God. Experiencing this love is what caused her to realize that God is so different from all the other gods. "His heart is not the same," she said with heartfelt gratitude. "I could feel that He was not angry with me for worshiping other idols. He knew I didn't know any better then; and step by step, He is leading me, even through the hard times."

基督教

Today, Ruth is focused on helping the Church in China prepare for cross-cultural missions. As a networker and facilitator, her role, as she sees it, is to connect with different churches, help them assess what they need to enact their missions vision and then help them fulfill their needs. The needs could involve a range of areas, from providing prospective missionaries with advanced Bible training to teaching about cultural awareness and helping to create sustainable business plans for livelihoods in the field.

In her own church, this also includes an emphasis on individual discipleship, which includes applying one's self to learning the Bible. Ruth appreciates the value that the Jewish people traditionally place on the study of God's Word and their reverence of His sovereignty, and she believes that, overall, the Church in China would do well to adopt a similar attitude. Based on her own spiritual journey to date, she feels strongly that this is an important concept for believers to grasp. Ultimately, "everything begins at home," she says, reiterating a key lesson she has learned from her divorce. "There needs to be harmony in the house. If there isn't, if there is disarray, this will have an impact on what one does outside of the home." Thus, she asks, "if individual church members are not properly nurtured in the faith—if they are not diligently followed up on—how will they be able to go out and be effective disciples themselves? And if there are no effective disciples, how will the Church have missionaries to send to the nations?"

It looks as if the message about discipleship and its value has been getting through as well. Ruth tells the story about how one member of the church, a young sister, recently shared a testimony at their Thanksgiving night about the healing she received. Four years prior, this lady had been a chronic sufferer of a nerve problem in her legs, which would periodically flare up and often cause her such intense pain and discomfort that she would hardly be able to walk. There were occasions when the episodes would get especially bad, causing her to be bedridden for days, sometimes even for weeks. The lady had been to visit doctors about the problem on numerous occasions and was tested for all sorts of illnesses, but the results always came back negative or inconclusive. There was no doctor who was ever able to give her a definitive diagnosis. All they could do was prescribe some painkillers and bed rest as needed.

As a new believer, this lady was hungry to know Jesus. But sometimes when the nerve pain broke out, it would leave her unable to attend church, and the disappointment and frustration she felt because of this only aggravated her physical discomfort. Ruth went to visit her during one such time. Moved with compassion for this younger sister, Ruth laid hands on her and prayed. She asked that the Lord would heal her sister from this condition so that she could come to church regularly to be discipled. Afterwards, Ruth left the sister and continued on with the rest of her day. In fact, she didn't give another thought to the prayer, and the event became another item on a long list of responsibilities that she had taken care of.

Fast-forward several years later to the recent Thanksgiving evening, where this same sister decided to stand up before the congregation and share what had happened in the interim. When she mentioned the nerve problem, Ruth suddenly remembered that she had prayed for this lady, and it was amazing to hear the results. The lady shared that since Sister Ruth had prayed for her that critical day, she had never once been rendered bedridden again from the condition. There had been some days that she felt like a nerve attack was coming on her legs, but she had never had to miss any more days of church or work because of it. In each of those testing times, she would call on the name of her Lord Jesus, in faith, and she would ask Him to continue to strengthen and heal her so that she could continue going to church to be discipled. The Lord was faithful, and He answered her prayer every time. As Ruth sat there listening, the woman's testimony was a revelation to her. *Yes, discipleship is important,* she thought, *but so is prayer.* It was an encouraging reminder to her of how powerful a tool prayer can be.

Over the years, Ruth has taken her fair share of business trips, and these have also shed further light on how the Church in China can achieve the goal of better missions preparedness. The trips have enabled her to observe the various individual challenges that confront a Chinese person when living overseas, as well as gain some understanding of the different cultures. In turn, this has helped her realize that churches need to be forming more realistic and suitable strategies for their missionaries as they prepare for their fields. She has also begun to envision her business exchanges becoming instrumental in forging key beachheads in the Back to Jerusalem quest. Even now she is building new inroads in one of the nations along the Silk Road. This came about as a result of a 40-day journey along the storied trading route.

In 2009, Ruth undertook the expedition in conjunction with a group of 15 leaders from various urban house churches around the country. The group was comprised of church pastors and leaders, businesspersons and a tour guide. The purpose of the trip was to begin, as she terms it, "the pioneering." Starting in the ancient capital of Xian, their convoy of four four-wheel-drive vehicles drove all the way from China to Israel via Pakistan, Iran, Turkey, Syria and Jordan. The leaders wanted to see the lay of the land, to touch and smell it for themselves, so that they could know precisely where and to what they were sending their missionaries.

Another factor that prompted the trip was the difficulties this group of leaders had learned of from the first wave of Chinese missionaries sent from the house churches in recent years to cross-cultural fields. Many of the 100 missionaries they spoke to reported that they were not receiving the financial support they had expected from their sending churches. When they tried to make ends meet for themselves, they were unable to generate enough income to cover the costs of living in their new lands.

Many of the missionaries also experienced grave loneliness and much frustration at what they perceived as a lack of fruit, which was not helped by the pressure of similar expectations back home to win new converts. People were simply not getting saved at the rate they were all accustomed to seeing in China. To make matters worse, many of the missionaries felt as though they had been abandoned in the field, or they were recalled to the Mainland, which led them to think they had failed. As far as they were concerned, they had lost face.

For the few who have remained at their posts, the thrust of their outreach at present is being directed toward migrant workers from China, hardly the cross-cultural harvest they had envisioned. Estimates are that there are currently hundreds of thousands of Chinese workers in Africa; hundreds of thousands more in the Middle East; and about 10,000 in Pakistan. (Border controls and records in many of these regions are somewhat lacking, which makes accurate figures hard to pin down.)

Until late 2009, there were also some 25,000 Chinese workers in India, but a change in the work visa laws of the world's second most populous nation forced thousands of the Chinese to leave. According to the Chinese Ministry of Commerce, there were a total of about 809,000 workers from the PRC overseas.[2]

The bulk of Chinese workers in Africa, the Middle East and the Indian subcontinent—all of which envelop significant portions of the celebrated silk trading routes—are hired as construction workers to build infrastructure such as railroads and power plants and buildings, or as laborers in the oil and gas or mining industries. It is not uncommon for accommodation to be provided for the Chinese workers, particularly if the contractor is owned by or has connections with the Chinese government. It is often the case that many of the migrants live in self-contained communities and have little interaction with the local population. Among other difficulties, the migrant workers often experience isolation and loneliness—the separation from their families by distance and time a costly price for each individual. The upshot is that there are plenty of needs among them to keep the few Chinese missionaries based in the area busy. As a result, the cross-cultural outreach goals continue to get put on hold; language study suffers, if it is happening at all; and there is little headway in getting to know and understand the local customs and people.

The 15 leaders who made the trip across the Silk Road route unanimously agreed that the Church in China needed to do a better job of preparing their missionaries for cross-cultural commissions. One of the prime motivations behind this trip, they said, was to begin finding solutions to the problems already identified. Missionaries who had returned were crying for help, and the Church could not ignore that. The question was, what could they do to prevent this situation from happening again? This question is especially acute for Ruth. She believes deeply that one of her roles is to help train and equip future missionaries. Therefore, she felt it was vital for her to go on this excursion to scout out the land.

The 40 days overland were eye-opening for the whole group. They knew they would encounter challenges along the way—that there would be much to learn; but they figured they could at least get through their native land without any problems. As it transpired, the biggest challenge actually came before they left home.

Abraham, who was one of the 15, recalled the difficulty of trying to exit the PRC. "We couldn't even cross the border from Xinjiang province into Pakistan," he said. "We all had visas to enter the next country, but our vehicles didn't. We didn't know we had to have permits for the cars to be driven in other countries."

What did they do?

"We had to fast and pray," Abraham said with a laugh. "This was so unexpected. We never imagined that China would have already given us the permission to leave but that we would be so unprepared to go in this basic way. We had nowhere to go!"

In fact, it took three intensive weeks of spiritual battle to get the all-important breakthrough at the first international border. The whole group participated in the fast and prayer. Some of them even decided to abstain from the Internet and video games. As a whole, the group never expected to get held up for as long as they did, but the weeks were not a waste. It turned out to be an invaluable time of forging greater team unity and bonding among all of the believers.

"All of these people have so many different ideas, and they are all used to leading," said Abraham. "So, at first it was very hard for us to gel together, to come to decisions that everyone could agree on. The other thing we needed," he said, "was to be made pure and holy for the trip. We needed to concentrate on God, to come before Him to make sure He would be with us on this trip. So those first few weeks were quite critical for each one of us."

Ruth agrees. "There were so many precious lessons from that journey. Of course there were the practical challenges, especially crossing the borders. But there were spiritual challenges, too, like our own holiness before God and our ability to work as a team. Iron sharpens iron—that was really true here."

"That trip helped us learn what fervent prayer really is," Abraham said, "what the whole process involves. As the Body of Christ, we need to understand this, and we really needed to learn the depth of what it means to truly accept one another so that each one of us could understand what God was saying to us in each country we went to."

Every country definitely felt different spiritually. "Some places were rich with God's blessings over the centuries, like Israel," Abraham said. "And Turkey was special for me, because it's from there, from Haran, that God called Abraham to leave his home and go to the place He had in mind for him."

Ruth recounted that there were "many, many miracles" throughout the journey, but for her, the one that stood out the most had to do with her own SUV. The vehicle was involved in an accident on one of the many rugged hillside roads in Pakistan, leaving the axle bent and the left front wheel twisted outwards. It was the middle of nowhere, which made it impossible to call a tow truck or a garage. As an experienced mechanic, though, Ruth knew that the extent of the damage sustained rendered the vehicle not worth fixing anyway; it would be better to scrap it. "In that moment, I heard the Lord say, 'Trust Me.'" So she radioed to the rest of the convoy to go ahead and continue on. She and her passengers were unharmed and would catch up with them.

After laying hands on the hood of the SUV and praying, Ruth decided to drive the vehicle. Amazingly, the SUV was able to continue on for the rest of the journey without further mechanical problems. Ruth was convinced that an angel held up the smashed area at the front, especially when locals along the way kept pointing to it as they drove by. Others would warn them not to drive it, whenever they paused to rest; but on they went. "I just believed in God," Ruth said.

Eventually, they made it all the way to Jerusalem, with Ruth's SUV racking up more than 3,500 kilometers after the accident! Ruth decided to ship her vehicle back to China, where a mechanic from one of her shops agreed with her assessment that it wasn't worth repairing. He was absolutely astounded that she had driven all that way given the condition of the vehicle. "God was lifting up that side of the car while you were driving," she recalls that her mechanic said. "If that's not a miracle, I don't know what is."

Delving deeper, Ruth believes that the difficulties the group faced on the trip were ultimately a reflection of those difficulties faced by the missionaries themselves. "It was all part of the process of growing into a stronger and more effective team unit."

Throughout the trip, the group's lack of vehicle permits led to repeated periods of fasting and praying. It took at least one day of spiritual battling before they were able to cross any of the borders between nations. But on the whole, the team felt it was time well spent with God, in light of the larger missions vision the Church in China was trying to fulfill.

基督教

Ruth came back from the trip greatly encouraged. She could more clearly see a whole new realm of possibilities that had only been mere concepts in her mind. Business, indeed, could be a very useful tool in the hands of the Lord. The natural networking that occurs through normal business dealings could be a means for God to open doors to meet key contacts in a new country, which in turn could lead the way to establishing a new business there. Furthermore, creating a business could be one way for missionaries to feasibly live in their new location and also relieve the financial burden on sending churches, the vast majority of which are still poor despite the PRC's growing economy and increasing wealth.

Her view is supported by the fact that a change in market trends can already be seen in Africa. Following on the coattails of the PRC government's multibillion-dollar projects in the construction, petroleum and mining industries, many ordinary Chinese citizens have chosen to pursue the profitable opportunities those headlining deals have presented by relocating themselves and plying their trades in the region. In some areas of the African continent, it is now estimated that as many as 80 percent of Chinese companies are small- or medium-sized enterprises.[3]

When done in the right and proper way, Ruth believes that a Chinese missionary in business could also be a valuable contributor to a local economy by providing jobs and services for the local people. One prospect that had crossed her mind, perhaps not surprisingly, was to open a chain of auto repair shops. It would be an excellent way, for instance, for a missionary to earn a living yet still allow for daily opportunities to meet and interact with the local people. It would also be a useful service and a way of contributing to the neighborhood.

Many of the regions where the Church in China plans to send missionaries do not have a natural affinity for Christianity. The dominant faiths are Islam and Hinduism. Hence, to go in and openly plant a church would not be an acceptable reason for many immigration departments to grant a work or residency visa. In some places, constructing a church building is not even legal. These harvest fields, to use the modern missions phrase, would be considered creative access countries. The techniques employed in spreading the gospel in these regions would have to be similar to those used in China 30 years ago—that is, without the help of formal church services, church buildings or Bible seminaries. It would have to be achieved through the course of daily living and all the interactions with people that daily life brings, including hosting people in their homes.

To Ruth's thinking, business and outreach go hand in hand. They are easily complementary. She also believes that forming strategic partnerships is necessary in some of the nations they are targeting. Partnering with the local church would be helpful for the Chinese Christians to adapt to their new language and culture, for example—a key area of failure identified by the first wave of missionaries. Most of these missionaries were so busy just trying to survive that they didn't have time to study a new language.

In return, the local believers and their outreach efforts could benefit from the help of the Chinese, who could bring in technology, resources or knowledge that the local believers may not have access to. "At the end of the day," Ruth says, "why reinvent the wheel if you don't have to? We are all living for a higher purpose, for a greater Kingdom. We are all on the same team."

Strategic partnerships are already being activated. The 40-day journey in 2009 brought Ruth into contact with local Christians in the nation of Pakistan. After a few follow-up visits, she has established some relationships. As of 2011, Pakistani Christians have begun to help some new Chinese missionaries learn Urdu and the customs of their land.

In another strategic partnership—one of the first of its kind—these same Chinese missionaries, who were commissioned to serve in the Muslim nation from the rural house church in China, are being supported financially by the urban church, namely Ruth's, during their period of language study. This is how this business-woman is responding to one of the vital lessons learned on unity from the 40-day overland journey.

"As Christians," said Ruth, "we should not be afraid to go anywhere. We should be bold, but we should also have humility to learn from our experiences and build on them. Then other people will be able to follow. Then will come a flourishing in the Lord. It's only then that we will be a blessing to people wherever we go.

"God is searching hearts," she continued. "He is testing the hearts of leaders. Many people have heard the call of God to serve, but not all of them have aligned themselves with His will. God is looking for a pure heart, for those who will follow Him com-pletely, wholeheartedly. There is no room for egos here, no room for superstars. We need to be very careful of our motives."

Ruth used to be a great planner in business. "I had to know where I was going," she said. "I had to know what I was going to do when I got there. But now, I just follow God's leading." The colonel's daughter explains that this is the lesson she learned from the book of Exodus when the Israelites followed the cloud of God's presence. "When the cloud moved, they moved. When it didn't, they didn't," she said simply. "The cloud moved with purpose and with timeliness.

"I really believe God will show me the way," she said with firm conviction. "I just need to follow Him. It's [a matter of] His will being done."

Notes

1. The Back to Jerusalem quest was originally envisioned in the early 1940s by a group of young Chinese evangelists and pastors, after the spread of the Shandong revival throughout China. Essentially the concept is that the spread of the gospel first began in Jerusalem. From there, over the centuries, it rolled out to the nations, circumnavigating the globe in a generally westward direction: Revivals came first to Europe and North America, which then led to missionaries carrying the good news to Africa, South America and then Asia. The only major regions that have not yet experienced revival are the nations between China and Israel. The Chinese Church believes they have been called to complete the circle and carry the gospel back to Jerusalem. As they follow the ancient Silk Road trading routes, the goal of the indigenous missions movement is to evangelize in each and every one of these predominantly Muslim and Hindu nations.

2. Zhao Yinan, "Outsource of Labor Tightened in China," *China Daily* (June 12, 2012).

3. Tessa Thorniley, "Big in Africa," *Danwei.org* (August 2, 2010).

2

"If You Build It, He Will Come"

*I once thought these things were valuable, but now I consider
them worthless because of what Christ has done. Yes,
everything else is worthless when compared with the infinite
value of knowing Christ Jesus my Lord. For his sake I have
discarded everything else, counting it all as garbage, so that I
could gain Christ and become one with him.*

PHILIPPIANS 3:7-9

PAUL FELT OFFENDED. And he wasn't one to offend easily. Yet it was true: He *did* feel an affront at what was being asked of him. He thought maybe he wasn't hearing right, so he shrugged the question off at first without much effort. But then he heard it again. And, again. He couldn't ignore it now. It was definitely his Father, and the filial piety ingrained in him since boyhood did not permit him to ignore the question any longer.

But why would his Father ask this of him? Surely He did not expect him to go into business. Paul turned the arguments over and over in his mind.

"You can't be serious," he said to the Lord yet again. "To be in business is to be secular. To be a merchant is to be immoral. Merchants are corrupt. They cheat. They scam. How could I stoop so low and do something like that?"

Since ancient times the merchant class has been looked down on by scholars and the nobility. According to the Confucian order of society, they ranked at the bottom of the hierarchy. This prejudice against businesspeople persisted all the way to the twentieth century, including through the first half of the Communist Party's 60-odd years of governing in the Mainland. So it wasn't surprising that Paul felt the request from his heavenly Father to be somewhat degrading.

Further reinforcing the unfavorable feelings he had toward trade and commerce was his disposition: Paul was someone who took pride in his heritage, that he was descended from a long line of Christians. In fact, he represented the seventh generation of believers in his family—a family whose vocations had only ever been honorable. His father, uncles, grandfathers and great-grandfathers had all been pastors, teachers or doctors. Businessmen? There were absolutely none among his ancestors. So, surely this was a misunderstanding.

The conversation between him and the Father about his profession had been going on for more than a year. (It was Paul, actually, who did most of the talking. God didn't have much to say after He made His request.) So either the perennial good boy was about to become a rebel, or he was going to have to own up to the fact that this was indeed what God wanted for him, and to act on it.

At the time, Paul, a lanky engineering graduate from a university in the city of Xiamen, was at the pinnacle of his career, as far as he was concerned. He was a researcher at his alma mater, specially invited and appointed to the position by the vice chancellor of the university. His was an esteemed position in society, a place that made perfect use of his gifts and that could be of benefit to others. Why should he give it up?

Especially, he continued debating with God, to do something he knew nothing about. "I don't know how to make deals," he argued back to his Father. "I can't lie—and isn't that what you have to do to make a sale? Please find someone else to do it."

God can be awfully silent after He's spoken. But Paul knew he was not going to win this argument, and it was not without some trepidation that he contemplated a future in business. He had good reason. He knew he was not naturally suited for deal making. He himself had been conned before, losing more than twice his annual salary in one instance alone. The loss caused him so much stress that his weight had dropped drastically, causing a friend to ask him if he was battling cancer.

In the end, Paul knew he would have to yield. He would have to trust. For in his heart he knew that above all else, he wanted to live a life that was pleasing to his Father.

$$基督教$$

It was during the construction boom in the 1990s that Paul opened the Xiamen En Pu Air Conditioning Equipment Company. The coastal city was benefiting from its designation as one of the PRC's first special economic zones (SEZ). A large influx of foreign investment led to buildings going up left, right and center. The whole eastern coastal region, in fact, of which Xiamen was a part, was on the receiving end of the lion's share of all foreign direct investment into the country—drawing 90.7 percent of FDI from 1983 to 1989, and a little more than 88 percent between 1990 and 1996.[1] Xiamen was entering the modern world at a rapid pace.

Known historically as Amoy, the city was the first port of trade used by the European traders who came to the Middle Kingdom in the sixteenth century. The city later became one of the treaty ports China opened in 1842, as a result of the First Opium War. The trading ships provided passage for some of the earliest Protestant missionaries to preach the gospel in the Mainland. Amoy was thus one of their earliest entry points, and the city claims China's first church in Xinjie Church, whose original structure was built by the Dutch Reformed Church of America in 1848.

In 1979, Xinjie was the first (Three Self) church reopened in Fujian province after the Cultural Revolution. It is a popular tourist attraction today. The tradition of commerce and trade would also resume in the southeastern port city with the founding of the Xiamen SEZ.

Paul's company became an agent for commercial air conditioning units sold in Fujian province. Various Western firms had approached him to sell their units, giving his company a unique position in the market since his products—whose brands included Carrier, Locke and McQueen—were made overseas. His company would provide sales, assembly and maintenance services for the machines in all of Fujian.

In the early to mid 1990s, air conditioners were not commonly found in Fujian buildings, neither in commercial nor residential. When Paul talked to his friends about the machines, mentioning the brand names, they all thought he was talking about a new kind of drink!

Initially, Paul was not totally convinced that he could sell these products. The first shipment cost several hundred thousand *renminbi*. He had just resigned his position at the university, which had paid him RMB200 per month—an average salary for his post at the time. So the commitment to invest several hundred thousand *renminbi* in the air conditioners and parts was a frightening amount of money to him. Nevertheless, he believed that this was what God wanted him to do. So, as he says, he just handed over his money to the suppliers. In return he received truckloads of product and naively asked his US partner if it would be all right for him to return the goods for a full refund if he couldn't sell them in six months.

Paul says that if it wasn't for God's grace, he doesn't know how he would have sold any of the machines. First of all, his products were considered high-end and expensive. It wasn't the traditional two- or three-story commercial-cum-residential development project that would be shopping for his goods; it was the still-uncommon contemporary skyscraper. Second, he did not behave like a typical local businessman. He did not possess the natural flair, instincts or desire to build *guanxi*, for example, the Chinese rendition of networking and making connections.

Moreover, he was seemingly not inclined toward providing quality customer service and had a habit of making clients wait on his schedule. As an example, he used to tell those who were ready to sign on the dotted line that he could not meet them for dinner that night because he had a "date" with Jesus.

Yet, he was acutely aware of his lack of deal-making savvy and was often extremely anxious about his ability to make the company profitable. Nevertheless, the inaugural shipment of air conditioners sold out completely before the six-month mark was up.

基督教

"God must really love me," says Paul. To this day he marvels at the fact that the company has not only managed to survive but is actually profitable and is now known in the industry across the province.

Just as the company grew over the years, so too did Paul's ministry to the church. Paul's numerous "dates" with Jesus were actually Christian gatherings at the homes of church members. For, in addition to running the air conditioning business, Paul was leading a house church that had several meeting points throughout the city and the surrounding area. In the 1990s, there were no formal churches with Sunday services outside of the Three Self Patriotic Movement, so he would lead Bible studies and encourage fellowship in these smaller and more casual settings virtually every night of the week.

Paul's Christian lineage and close proximity to those who have suffered for their faith—including his own father and grandfather, who were denounced and struggled against by the Red Guards during the Cultural Revolution—were defining factors in his employment of the house church model of worship in his own assembly. Having witnessed firsthand the confiscation of Bibles from his home as a child, which led to a brief involvement in Bible smuggling at one point in his younger years, Paul is a strong advocate of committing Scripture to memory. To this day, in his

Bible teaching, he continues to assign his students Scripture memory verses.

"It's difficult for someone to imagine how desperate the situation was," Paul said in reference to his emphasis on the Bible, "if he or she had not been through the Cultural Revolution." In fact, when he became a Christian in 1976, the year Chairman Mao died and the infamous revolution ended, there were no Bibles to be found. At that time, the Bible was an officially banned book. If Bibles were discovered by the Red Guards, they were confiscated and usually burned or destroyed by some other means.

Paul copied portions of Scripture by hand when he met other believers who were fortunate enough to have successfully hidden their whole Bible or a partial part of the book. "That's why," he says jokingly, "my Chinese character writing looks so nice today."

基督教

In 2002, God spoke to Paul about another career change. This time he asked Paul to give up the business to become a full-time pastor. Xiamen En Pu Air Conditioning Equipment Company was now seven years old and reputable. Moreover, the company's annual turnover, in the tens of millions of *renminbi*, enabled Paul to enjoy great personal wealth. He was even thinking of sending his son to university in the United States when he graduated from high school in a few years.

Paul wanted his son to have the best education that money could buy, but he had to admit there was an ulterior motive too. He felt like he owed his son something more, something special, and was attempting to alleviate his conscience somewhat. Between building up the business and the church over the years, Paul felt that he had neglected his son along the way. Both work and ministry commitments had consumed too many hours and, all too often, the best of his energy. He should have been a better father. He should have made more time to be with his son, to help him with his homework and just be there for him. So he hoped to make it up by enabling him to study at university abroad.

But now his plans were in jeopardy. If Paul did what God was asking of him, he would lose the considerable income that came along with his position in the company. The substantially lower salary of a Chinese pastor would not be enough to cover international student tuition fees. Complicating the matter, for several years now he had been sowing ideas into his son's mind of the benefits and advantages of receiving higher education overseas. Paul felt that he would be breaking a promise to the boy if he would no longer be able to afford to send him. He also felt like he was depriving his child of something good, thereby sacrificing his son's future in the process. What kind of father would do that if he could prevent it?

Despite the company's success, Paul had never really mastered the finer nuances or strategies of making investments and managing cash flow. In both his business and personal finances, he maintained a straightforward, practical, in-and-out view. As long as money was coming in, it could go out. There was no thought of saving for a rainy day or, for that matter, his son's American college fund. Neither was there a long-term business plan for the future of the company. Beyond ensuring that the firm was not in the red, his primary focus was to build up the church, to care for the flock's needs, both spiritual and physical. The company's unexpected profitability felt like a windfall to him—he had never had such easy access to so much money before—and he developed the habit of directing the bulk of his personal income toward meeting the needs of the church.

As on the previous occasion, when God had asked him to become a businessman, the conversation between Paul and his Father about this latest career change was a drawn-out affair. This time the mostly one-sided discussion lasted two years. Paul didn't like what he was hearing and he had to be sure it was right. To his mind, the Lord's direction did not seem logical. After all, wouldn't it make more sense if he just kept on running the company so that the church could keep on benefiting? He didn't even keep the wealth for himself—only enough for the needs of his family. The rest went to the church.

Members of his congregation who were migrant workers, for instance, would need some kind of assistance from time to time when their move to the city meant that they often lost access to the subsidized housing, health care, unemployment insurance and free education for their children that they would automatically have back home in their village. (The country's *hukou*, or residency, system determines where people can access social services and benefits. If an individual and his family move away from their designated residency, the consequence is usually the loss of access to those services. In effect, the individual—and any family members he or she happens to bring along—often ends up living like a second-class citizen within his own country, encountering not only social exclusion but discrimination and, at times, even loss of self esteem as well.)

Paul couldn't ignore those kinds of practical needs, not when he had the means to help. It was true that, in general, household incomes and standards of living were rising in the country, but the reality was that there were many, many more people in China who were still struggling to make ends meet. His church members were faithful in their giving, but it was his salary that covered most of the assembly's rental, administration and operating costs.

By the beginning of 2004, the church had begun running a regular Sunday service, including a Sunday School for children, in addition to the weeknight meetings in homes. As well as gathering members from the different house groups, the church initially attracted local families from the city. Later on, it saw its composition change to also include migrant workers and university students from other parts of the country. The lone Sunday service eventually expanded, and today there are five meetings spread over the weekend, with two family services and a meeting geared toward students and workers from out of town on Sunday, as well as two meetings for young adults and singles on Saturday.

Signs and wonders in the fellowship are not unheard of. The Cai family is a prime example. Paul shares the story of how they came to be among those who joined the original Sunday service in 2004 as a result of experiencing a wonderful healing.

Mr. and Mrs. Cai had an 18-year-old son back then, who was out riding his motorcycle one day when he was hit by a mini-bus. It was a wonder the young man survived the crash at all. Nevertheless, he suffered a severe traumatic brain injury from the accident and lay in a coma for more than two months. He eventually woke up, but remained in a persistent vegetative state. The parents were totally crushed. He was their one and only son, and they were desperate to see him well again. They called in the Daoist shamans, who performed rituals, chanted incantations and concocted an array of potions that were fed to their son via his feeding tube. It was all to no avail though. His vegetative state continued.

A neighbor, who had compassion on the family and who "co-incidentally" happened to be a member of Paul's church, told the Cais about Jesus and His healing power. He asked them if they would be willing to allow him and his church to come and pray for their son. Initially, the parents were hesitant. They worried that if they believed in Jesus it would offend the Daoists. Eventually, because nothing else was helping, they decided to let their neighbor and his church friends come pray.

Mr. and Mrs. Cai noticed right away that the Christians were different: To begin with, when they came into the Cai home, they didn't ask for or accept any "lucky money" in red packets. Nor did they require any other kind of payment or preparations from the family in exchange for their prayers. They saw only loving-kindness from the believers toward their son and themselves.

It was especially moving for the parents when the Christians asked if they could actually stand beside their son's bedside and hold his hand. They weren't afraid of all the medical machines and tubes around him, and they were not repulsed by the sickly smell that permeated his bedroom, as many other visitors had been.

This won Mr. Cai over, who decided that he would like to visit the church. One visit turned into a few more, and Mrs. Cai could not help but notice how her husband seemed somehow different after coming home from the services. A sense of despair was no longer constant around him, and he seemed somehow hopeful. Eventually, she overcame her own skepticism and decided to accompany her husband to the church, where the couple committed themselves to believe in Jesus Christ. Afterwards, even though their son still lay in his bed, the two of them daily experienced a rich, incredible joy with their Savior.

The Christians came to pray regularly for the Cais' son, including Paul. After more than half a year in a persistent vegetative state, something extraordinary happened: The son began following the voices of the people in the room with his eyes. He became increasingly aware of his surroundings, and then he began to turn his head. Gradually, in time, as he gained more physical strength, he slowly started to speak again and move his hands, arms and upper body. It was a sheer delight to see him able to sit up in bed again.

The next thrill came when he began to move his legs. At long last, the unforgettable day came when he could stand once more! It was a miracle! To this day the son continues to gain strength, and he is able to walk supported by a frame. Everyone in the neighborhood heard the marvelous news and was astonished! At least 10 different families ultimately came to know the Lord because of this awe-inspiring healing.

Today, Paul's church has more than 600 members. Because of its size and continuing growth, it has unavoidably come to the attention of the local government. As a result, the church has moved location several times over the last few years in an effort to minimize official notice.

But in January 2004, Paul didn't know that the 60-odd people would multiply by more than 10, or that the lone Sunday meeting would expand to include more gatherings over the entire weekend. The only thing he knew was that he would no longer have the means to send his son overseas for university. This, along with practical concerns about maintaining the church, was the major weight on his mind.

His decision would hinge on the answers to these two questions. "Our church does not have rich people," he would say to God. "It's me who pays the bills. Who will then pay them if I earn only a pastor's salary?" When he heard the still, small voice within him answer, "I'll pay the bills," Paul did not believe it. All he saw was that the church would have no money. "So surely," he would argue back, "it would be better for me to remain as president of the company so that more people could be blessed."

Things came to a head six months later, in the Garden of Gethsemane. Paul and his wife were visiting Israel for the first time. On a group tour in the Holy Land, the caravan of buses filled with Chinese Christians came to a stop at the famous place where Jesus prayed on the night He was arrested, just before His crucifixion. Earlier in the day, the couple had been enjoying the fellowship at a Christian conference whose attendees included Chinese believers from all over the world, and this tour stop was expected to build upon the edifying experiences they had been having so far.

As Paul walked among the olive trees and flower beds, he became unusually overwhelmed with emotion. There was an indelible moment when he looked forward and could no longer see the tourists meandering through the vegetation; instead he saw a picture of Christ praying in the garden. His Lord was kneeling there, yielding Himself to His Father's will. The picture gently faded. Paul hung his head in shame. He was convicted, and he began to weep. Completely overcome, his sobs and tears gushed forth like a torrent, and try as he might, he could not stop them.

Some in the group began to wonder at this pastor who was unable to control his emotions. His wife handed him some tissues to wipe his tears. He used them up. She then gave him the rest of her pack. He used those up too. Now the people around him began to dig into their bags and fish out their Kleenex for him. Gratefully received, those were soon soaked through as well. And still others gave him more.

In the middle of the garden he felt he could no longer put off what God had been asking him to do. He knelt there and committed himself to pastor the church full time. He would resign his position at the air conditioning company. "But," he said to the Lord, "I ask only one thing: Let my son be willing to stay in China for his university studies since I will not be able to afford to send him overseas."

Upon his return to China, Paul never stepped foot in his office again. When he called the vice president of his company and informed him that he would no longer be working there, he was not believed. Nevertheless, Paul was true to his word. A month later, upon noticing that his boss still hadn't showed up, the vice president had Paul's office cleared out.

Paul also had a heart-to-heart talk with his son, who understood and supported his father's decision. Today Paul's son is studying at a university in Xiamen and will soon graduate with a bachelor's degree.

基督教

The church has not only grown in numbers over the years, but it has also seen the signs and wonders continue to flow. "We have so many miracles," Paul said, when asked about them. "I don't even know which one to tell you about." But the telling of one story is inspired soon enough when he notices a delightfully pretty, doll-like toddler playing at the side in his church. She is three years old, and her name, when translated from the Chinese, means "Proclaiming Grace."

In the first place, Grace isn't supposed to be alive. She shouldn't even have been conceived. In the days before she became a Christian, Grace's mother had led a rather loose life and, as a result, she had had five abortions. The last time the procedure was done, she was informed that she would no longer be able to have a child.

In due course, Grace's mother came to the knowledge of God's saving grace, and she went on to marry a Christian man who happened to be a member of Paul's church. Naturally, the couple wanted to raise a family, but nine years into their marriage, there were no children.

The man and wife then entered midlife, and they each faced physical challenges of their own. She, of course, was still unable to conceive due to the effects of her past life; while he, on the other hand, suffered recurring pain and discomfort from a vertebral defect he was born with and that left him with a hunched back as an adult. Nonetheless, the two grew in their faith and they believed in their God's ability to give life, so they asked Paul and his wife to pray for them to be able to have a child. How could Paul and his wife refuse? So by faith, they prayed, and several months later they received their answer: The lady's womb had been healed and it was confirmed that she had conceived!

A few months into the pregnancy they faced a new battle for Grace's life. The expectant parents had gone to the hospital for a prenatal checkup that included an ultrasound scan. They received the most devastating news. The medical staff told them that the scan revealed that the fetus was deformed. The doctor proceeded to lay out the options before them. If the parents chose to carry the baby to term, it would be born disfigured and disabled. Therefore, he highly recommended that they abort the baby. Sensing their hesitation, the nurses supported their colleague's advice and strongly urged them to abort. Why would you want to make your child and yourselves go through such a hard life, they asked?

But the husband and wife firmly believed that God had extraordinarily answered their prayers in allowing the conception to happen in the first place. This naturally led to their unswerving conviction that He would not want this pregnancy to end in death. Besides, how could the doctor and nurses possibly expect them to allow their child to be killed? It was an unthinkable idea! So they went back to church and asked Paul and his wife for advice and to pray for their baby—that it would be delivered safely and be healthy.

The pastor and his wife shared their heartbreak, yet it didn't change the fact that the results of the scan seemed so certain and the choice before the couple was hard. What could Paul and his wife possibly say to override the results of this medical test? *Sure, God can heal,* Paul thought to himself, *but would He really do so here? Hadn't He already performed a miracle in allowing the woman to conceive? Could they really expect Him to perform another one?* This new mountain seemed even higher to the pastor than the last one. It would surely be a huge test of faith to overcome this.

"To tell you the truth, I wasn't feeling that confident about prayer being enough," Paul admitted. "I was secretly hoping that no one else in the church knew about the bad report from the hospital so that no one would be disappointed if the prayers we were about to say were not answered."

Upon further discussion, however, Paul discovered that the couple had already been mobilizing the troops in the church and asking them to intercede for their child. Paul sighed inwardly. What else could he do? There was no way he could just say the obligatory prayer and then hope the whole problem would go away and no longer be his responsibility. There was going to be a life or death battle whether he wanted it or not. The only question now was, would he be a part of it or not? If he chose not to be a part, what kind of example of faith would he, as the leader of the church, demonstrate? How would it look if everyone else was willing to persevere in prayer and faith in this circumstance, but the pastor was not? *This should not be,* he said to himself.

Paul knew what he had to do. "I gathered the whole church," he recalled, "and announced that we would be holding a special time of fasting and prayer for the baby and the couple." The pastor had taken up his position, and the fervent attitude of prayer continued throughout the remainder of the pregnancy.

Grace came into the world two months prematurely. She weighed in at only two-and-a-half pounds and was kept in an incubator for two months in the children's intensive care unit. During that time, neither mother nor father was allowed to hold or even visit their child. But the father was unmovable in his faith: He believed that their new daughter would be all right. Every day he diligently wrote out on a sheet of paper a different promise from the Word of God. He then asked his daughter's nurse if she would please read this Scripture aloud to his child and then lay it on top of her cot afterwards. While not a Christian herself, the nurse was kind enough to carry out the father's request.

Meanwhile, the church kept a prayer vigil going for Grace's life in the hall outside of the ICU, with individual members taking turns in half-hour shifts to do spiritual battle throughout the day. A couple of months later, Grace had gained sufficient weight and was deemed healthy enough by the hospital to go home. Today, with no disabilities or disfigurements, she is flourishing, lively, active and, in Paul's words, "a true miracle child!"

Miracle children seem to be common in Paul's church. The pastor then went on to tell another story, this time about a six-year-old boy. Several years before he was born, his mother, a medical doctor, had gone to study for a doctor of philosophy degree at a university in Hong Kong. As part of her course, she had been required to conduct scientific experiments in a lab. During one of those experiments, she suffered an unfortunate accident that exposed her to radioactive materials. This exposure led to her developing a number of long-term health problems.

She saw a dramatic increase in her white blood cell count, for instance. As a medical practitioner, she knew that if she should ever become pregnant, it would be dangerous for her, given her now weakened health. Beyond that, there would in all likelihood be consequences for her child as well. A very real possibility existed that any child of hers would suffer from severe ongoing health problems or physical deformities. There would also be a higher risk of any child of hers developing cancer at a later stage in his life, should he make it there.

One day, when her studies were over and she was living back in the Mainland, she discovered that she had become pregnant. What had previously been an intellectual thought process for her had now become a genuine dilemma: Should she go through with the pregnancy or not? Without a doubt her doctor advised that she should have an abortion. It was in her best interests. Her health was compromised. Why put her own life at risk by trying to have a baby? All of the medical voices around her were saying the same thing, including her peers in Xiamen, Fuzhou and Shanghai. As far as they were all concerned, there was no other option but to abort. The pressure was intense.

She also had to consider that apart from the worries about saving her own life, to carry to term would be to risk birthing a child who would have to endure endless physical struggles throughout his life, as well as the mental anguish of being stigmatized by the bulk of Chinese society, or living in lonely isolation. (Chinese culture is such that deformed or disabled persons are usually viewed as shameful. Families with "abnormal" members traditionally tend to keep them hidden at home or away in remote places, far from the public eye.)

To make matters worse, the early signs in her pregnancy were not good. One of her prenatal scans showed a complication: Her umbilical cord was twisted in knots, and the baby was not being nourished properly. It seemed to be further proof that she should definitely expect her baby to be disabled.

In her heart, she felt that she could not allow her baby to be killed. It just did not seem to be the right choice. Her husband agreed with her. The more they both thought and prayed about it, the more they believed she should see the pregnancy through. They believed by faith that God had meant for this life to exist. So who would they be, then, to end his life? They determined then and there that she would give birth to this child, come what may.

Nine months passed, and by faith, their son was born. He was underweight and unhealthy looking. After checking the newborn over, the doctor announced that the infant had a defective heart as well as a nonfunctioning kidney and pancreas, among other problems. The atmosphere after the delivery was heavy and depressing. All the signs indicated that this child would not survive long in this world. Even if he did manage to make it through his first year and go on to grow up, he would most likely be severely disabled.

The new parents did not waver in their faith. They lovingly took their newborn to church, and everyone gathered around the new family to pray for them, especially for the child. During the next year the church also faithfully sent teams to the family's home to continue the prayer ministry.

The boy's first birthday came. He had made it after all. The one-year-old was then taken to the hospital for another medical check-up. This time the doctors and nurses could not find any problems with his heart, kidney, pancreas or any other part of his body. He was not deformed in any way that they could see. It was incredible to them! The child was completely healed! Today the boy is a very healthy, active and intelligent student in primary school.

Paul says that the prayer teams have been a key factor in the continued flow of miracles they have been seeing in their church. He believes the ministry of prayer does not rest on just one or two people in a church, or on the pastors or an elite few. This contrasts, however, from what he has seen throughout the course of his international travels. The pastor from Xiamen has noticed that many healing ministries outside of China tend to promote a sole "faith healer" or "miracle worker." This is a style of ministry, he believes, that would never be able to get off the ground in the PRC. It is an approach that would not be tolerated by the officials for very long.

"If anyone ever tried to position himself or portray himself like that here," he says rather bluntly, "the local authorities would most likely close him down very, very quickly." He believes that the whole church should be taught (and it is taught in his) to be totally involved and engaged in prayer. It is one way that people are able to see the fruit of their faith in action and realize for themselves that they are indeed a valuable part of the Body of Christ. Each one can make a difference.

基督教

"God's grace is free," says Paul. "If you want to receive blessings, though, there are conditions. It's not enough for Christians to only hear or know about God's Word. We have to put what we hear and know into action. We need to be living it, demonstrating it through our lives."

Paul's comments are derived from his observations of Chinese society in recent years and, more specifically, his concerns that unhealthy habits are increasingly creeping into people's lifestyles and having an adverse effect on them. Obesity, for example, has become a health problem, particularly in the cities. The simple truth is that more and more city dwellers are becoming less physically active while overeating and consuming less nutritional foods. Officially, there are 100 million obese people in China, thanks in part to the proliferation of fast food and other international brands, particularly in urban areas. Some predict that figure could double within five years.[2]

While there are red flags in regard to the potential health problems that arise from the gluttony, the same can also be true for the spiritual wellbeing of people. Strong and mature Christians do not simply pop out of the oven overnight. The fruit of the Spirit takes time to grow in a person. Yet the scale and the speed of change in society, which have mounted even more pressure in people's lives, have led to an attitude of resignation and mere following after the latest trends.

Sometimes the result is that people do not truly understand what they are getting into. In terms of Christianity, while it is always positive when people want to commit their lives to Jesus, Paul cannot help but feel misgivings about the quality of faith today in some of these new converts, and their capacity to mature. He fears that their faith is under threat of being diluted and their growth stunted. In his opinion, the biggest challenge facing the Church in China today is that they will simply become "Sunday Christians."

"Many people claim to be Christians," he says. "But when you hear them talk about their values and see their world view, you realize they are actually very materialistic. Their spiritual understanding is not very deep, and there is not much devotion to Christ." Paul believes that the reason for the widening shallowness and immaturity of faith is that many people do not read the Bible and, therefore, do not understand the Father's heart.

To combat this, Paul regularly emphasizes in his own teaching the value and importance of the Bible for every Christian. He talks about it in team-building sessions with his church leaders and when lecturing for Bible schools. At home, for his own church, Paul has prescribed a daily devotional regimen—one that requires real commitment to maintain. Not only does each believer follow a set schedule of Bible readings, but he or she is also expected to journal extensively about the daily reading.

The program was first tested for six months by his team of 46 leaders before fanning out to the rest of the church in 2010. Similar to Ruth's views on individual discipleship, Paul says that if the leaders don't do it, the congregants won't. Everything starts at home or, in this case, at the top.

The program was not an easy sell to his leaders. Some complained that the reading and journaling were too time consuming. Each day's assignment required at least an hour to complete thoroughly. Others said that their blood pressure was rising because of the amount of work it entailed. Paul laughs as he remembers the objections and protests from the team. But he held firm and encouraged his team to persevere.

Over a period of time, he saw fruit that pleased him. The leaders were beginning to mature, and this made it easier to roll out the plan to the rest of the church. The ones who complained about higher blood pressure even reported that after a few weeks it returned to normal.

基督教

Declining morals in Chinese society also weighs on Paul's heart. Wealth and material possessions may be accumulating in the country, but moral standards are falling. Paul believes that the onus is on the leadership of the Church to show the way. "If Christian leaders don't uphold the standards, and if we don't demonstrate how Christians should be living, how will the rest of the church know how to live?"

Looking at his own church, for example, he senses that many members are walking a fine line between trying to honor their parents' wishes and endeavoring to measure up in their ever-changing world. Approximately two-thirds of Paul's congregation is from out of province, with the majority of them unmarried. In terms of gender, there are more women than men in the church. If they are factory girls come to work in the coastal region's many plants, there is the deep-seated filial obligation to regularly send money home, support the family and, eventually, get married. If they are university students come to study in one of the nation's more advanced cities, the peer pressure is on for girlfriends to live with their boyfriends, and from parents, who expect their children to excel in their studies and achieve top grades to secure the best career options.

Paul's wife sheds further light on some of the challenges the women face. "Of course the single women want to find a husband," she says. "And of course they want him to be a Christian. But finding a truly committed and mature Christian husband is very hard because the churches in China have almost always had more sisters than brothers. Some of our single women are in their thirties, and the pressure from their parents is unrelenting. 'Why do you believe in God?' they ask. 'If God is so good, why can't he give you a husband?'"

Why are there not more Christian young men?

"There are a few reasons," Paul answers. "First, there is tremendous family pressure on sons to have successful careers and make money. The men then tend to get distracted or lost in those pursuits, especially if they live in the cities.

"Another reason is that men and women are just different in their makeup. Chinese men don't let go of themselves emotionally. They're more reserved. Women, on the other hand, tend to be more in touch with their feelings and aren't afraid to show them. They're generally more expressive and talkative, and that naturally leads them into sharing the gospel with other women.

"Finally," Paul concludes, "there is a perception among men that Christianity is for women and children. It is not masculine. If the man comes from a rural area, for instance, the perception is that back in the village, the people who believe in God are usually old ladies, or they can't read and write. So he tends to already have this idea in his mind that Christians are geriatric and ignorant, and therefore he has no interest in attending church once he moves to the city."

基督教

Looking ahead, Paul hopes, like Ruth, that his church will one day become a missionary-sending church. When he was growing up in the faith, he was blessed with opportunities to learn from overseas pastors who came to Xiamen to teach the Bible and demonstrate genuine unconditional love. "There's a cost in going," he says, "and they paid it." Borrowing from their example, Paul says that the Church in China ought to pass on what it has learned. That's the whole spirit behind missions: giving, passing it on. "If a church is healthy," he believes, "if it is having true revival, a natural by-product should be that missionaries are sent out. It should be a church that passes on what it has received."

One way he sees this happening in his own church is through the majority of congregants who originate from out of the province. Paul tells the story of a co-worker who came from Jiangxi province to learn and work alongside him in Fujian for a time. The co-worker saw firsthand how Paul pastored his church—from building up his leadership team to managing practical, everyday matters that arose. He also saw how Paul carefully prepared for short ministry trips to more remote and poorer rural areas to provide Bible teaching to churches with less access and means for extra resources and materials to facilitate their church growth. These churches had asked Paul if he would be willing to come, even though it meant taking him away from his own church for a while; and the co-worker saw that he willingly did so. With these lessons in his heart, the co-worker has since returned to Jiangxi and begun his own church, which today has more than 150 people. It thrills Paul, and he hopes "to hear more testimonies like this in the future," he says with a smile.

Missions, Paul has discovered, is not just about giving blessings to others. When he does go on the short ministry trips in the more destitute areas of the country, to give or pass on what he has received, he finds that he is the one who actually receives the blessing. It is not uncommon on these trips for Paul to drive 8 to 10 hours to get to his destination, then minister and teach from the Bible virtually nonstop for 9 or 10 hours during each of the next three days. He will then get back into his car and drive all day to get to the next place. There he will go through the whole ministry and teaching process again with another group of equally hungry believers.

"These people only have a plank of wood to sit on," he says. "They have no chairs. But they have a great hunger for God. In the countryside, especially in the remote and poorer areas, the churches sometimes don't have full-time pastors, or there is less opportunity for them to receive extra Bible teaching. They are glad to have these meetings, and they are very focused in them. Now, if I were to speak for 10 hours at my church, the people would have gone home a long time ago! They can no longer accept such long teaching sessions. So these trips are actually a true blessing to me. I think I'm more blessed than the students I'm teaching."

Paul believes that in missions the most important thing is to have a burden or a heart for the lost. "It's even more important than having the training," he says. "When you have the burden, you will then have the desire to do what it takes to reach the lost—get the training, gain the qualifications, study or whatever else. We've got to go and give."

Upon further thought, Paul realizes that the Church in China doesn't yet have enough missionaries. "Look at the South Korean Church," he says. "They've set a very good example of sending many missionaries abroad. They've motivated many people to go. We haven't done that yet. We need to learn from their example."

Using a favorite analogy of his, Paul likens the Church in China to the golden lampstand in the Bible. In the time of Moses, the golden lampstand was made out of one piece of gold, hammered and beaten into its shape by a craftsman. The function of the end product, obviously, was to give light; and in so doing, to influence its surroundings. The Church in China has been hammered and beaten through her years of persecution, he says. It has been refined as gold. But ultimately she is here to influence her community, her city and her world. That's the testimony of the Church, he asserts. And that's the type of church this pastor from Xiamen is endeavoring to build.

Notes
1. China State Statistical Bureau, quoted in Huang Ping and Zhan Shaohua, *Internal Migration in China: Linking It to Development*; Regional Conference of Migration and Development in Asia, Lanzhou, China, March 14-16, 2005.
2. "Obesity Rates Soar in China with Greater Wealth," *FoxNews.com*, January 1, 2010.

3

To Immigrate or Not?

*I had only heard about you before, but now I have seen you
with my own eyes.*

JOB 42:5

THE LETTER WAS OFFICIAL. He could hardly believe it. Yet there it was staring back at him: The government of Australia had approved Job and his wife's applications to immigrate to the land Down Under. After a year and a half of undergoing skill assessments, English language tests, health and medical check-ups and a police clearance, they had finally gained their residency visas. They could finally leave all the chaos, pollution and backwardness that were in China and give their son the chance to have a better quality of life.

Then an old friend arrived in town for a visit. She and Job's wife had been classmates at school back in the day, and she had moved to Australia a few years earlier. The timing of her visit back to the PRC couldn't have been better, as far as Job and his wife were concerned. Now they had the perfect opportunity to find out exactly what they needed to know before they moved to their new country.

Much to her surprise, Job's wife quickly lost interest in what her friend had to say. All her friend talked about was Jesus and how her life was new and so different since she had moved to Australia. This made Job's wife feel that actually she was quite content with her life. She didn't need so much newness. She also didn't need religion, thank you very much. Was that all she would have to look forward to in her new country—going to church on Sundays and reading the Bible the rest of the week? That sounded boring! Her friend had never been superstitious when they were at university.

Somewhat reluctantly, Job had to agree with his wife. Life in Australia didn't sound very exciting after all. But beyond the friend's description, there was something in what she was saying. It was as if Job had heard those words before. He searched the recesses of his mind and then remembered. It was a conversation in passing with a foreigner several years back. At the time, Job had thought that he, as a doctor, was offering nothing more than polite chitchat to fill the silence while he treated the man's daughter's injured hand. As he was stitching her wound, Job had asked the father, "Why did you come to China? Why would you leave the good life in the United States to come here? It's so poor." "Because," the American had replied, "China needs to be saved."

China needs to be saved. Job felt the shock and wonder of those words again. What in the world had this American to do with China? He wasn't even of Chinese descent! Yet, he chose to come and live here. Job marveled once more at the depth of commitment and love the man had expressed for his Jesus, that he was willing to do something like that. The man *and* his family were willing even though China was beggarly compared to the place they came from. Even though it was not as advanced or convenient. Even though he didn't know the language or the customs, and he had to learn about them. The man had come to help *save* China! The thought staggered Job.

For several days afterward that conversation wouldn't leave him. His mind just could not comprehend it. Was this Jesus someone so worth following? Was it within the realm of possibility that His love could be so real and so rich? Were the words this man and his wife's friend had spoken the truth? With sobering clarity, Job felt a challenge emerge from within: If a foreigner can live in China, why can't he?

基督教

It could be said that Job's desire to leave China was inherent. It was arguably already in his blood. He had an uncle on his father's side who had won funding, in the 1940s, from Tsinghua University, to do advanced study in the United States. Subsequently, he enrolled at the University of Michigan and studied thoracic surgery under Dr. John Alexander, a pioneer in the specialist field.

When China underwent upheaval with the Sino-Japanese war, the uncle discovered that he was a patriot at heart. He could have chosen to remain in the United States after completion of his studies. He even turned down a job offer at a hospital with a monthly salary of US$3,000—an amount at that time that was only to be dreamed of by most Chinese. Instead, after four years abroad, he chose to return home in 1945 to help build the country.

According to *The Annals of Thoracic Surgery*, Dr. Huang Si, as he is more commonly know in China, was a "great surgeon" and "an inspiring mentor and leader of the younger generations of surgeons in China." His medical textbook on surgery, which is named after him, went through multiple reprints and is still used in medical schools in the PRC. Job's uncle is the only Chinese doctor to be elected as one of the 228 founding members of the American Board of Thoracic Surgery. When he passed away in 1984, the American Medical Association had a bust of the thoracic surgeon made and sent to his home village in Jiangxi province (though the gift from overseas was declined by the Chinese government, who eventually erected their own statue of the doctor in a local park).

Australia was not the first place that Job and his wife had tried to immigrate to. Shortly after they were married, in 1993, they had applied to move to Canada. The events of Tiananmen Square in 1989, the year Job finished his university studies and began his medical practicum, had left their scars on the minds of the young idealistic couple, and they hoped to be able to live in a place without such uncertainty or fear of the future.

Once again, friends who were already in the "promised land" proved to have an influential voice. Ultimately, Job and his wife were discouraged by their stories of how hard it was to adapt to life in the Great White North. How was it that a professor of nuclear physics at a university in China could only find a job washing dishes in a restaurant in his new homeland? They had moved so that they could have a *better* life. But it wasn't better, and so Job and his wife had decided to withdraw their Canadian applications.

Job asked himself, *Why was a foreigner willing to live in China, but he was not?* The question nagged at him. It was not logical to his mind. As an orthopedic surgeon, he was used to explanations that could be proven and backed up by research, even if he had to undertake the study himself. He therefore decided to investigate this Jesus and learn what he could about Christianity. He wanted to know who Jesus was and why He mattered.

Job knew that Christians went to church, so he figured that the local Three Self Patriotic Movement church was a good place to start. He had actually visited a TSPM church after the Tiananmen Square crackdown, in an attempt to search for some answers after the tragedy. That time he did not hear anything of help or interest to him. Nevertheless, the TSPM church was an easy place to find and was approved by the government. There would be no harm in trying once more. Maybe he hadn't given the TSPM an honest hearing before.

As he sat in the meetings now, he compared what he was hearing with what his wife's friend and the foreigner had said. It was not the same. The TSPM was saying that justification came by love and works. A good, devout Christian, according to the TSPM, was someone who had love and undertook to perform good works. These were the main criteria for a believer to be accepted by God.

His wife's friend and the foreigner, on the other hand, had said that there was nothing anyone could do to earn the love and acceptance of Jesus. He gave it freely to those who believed, and people were justified in God's eyes because of their faith in Jesus. It seemed to the doctor that the TSPM only emphasized doing the right thing—the acts of good deeds were the only thing that mattered. It sounded like a mere ritual. Where was the faith in that? Where was the hope? *I may as well go to a*

Chinese temple and burn incense, Job thought to himself. He was disappointed by what he heard in the TSPM and decided not to go back there.

Next he decided to try a house church. This was harder to find, but now that he had begun his search, he had to finish it. He couldn't leave the questions unanswered. In fact, he had even more questions now after his visits to the TSPM. Eventually, Job and his wife found a fellowship group through a friend. The Bible studies and discussions were lively affairs and often turned into spirited debates on all kinds of topics, including other religions, such as belief in traditional Chinese gods, the supernatural realm, and more. This was ideal for Job. He could lay all his questions out on the table. Nothing was taboo. And here he found a difference: Somehow, in answering his many questions, the words of the Christians seemed to be alive. They would click with something inside him, and he felt them deeply. There was, he perceived, truth in them.

The solemn realization that dawned on Job over the course of time was that his hope in life had been in the wrong place. Where once all he could see were the problems and pollution, his hope now was in the saving grace of his Lord Jesus Christ. He knew he no longer had to leave China to find a better life.

基督教

The decision to give up the immigration dream continues to flummox some in the West. "Us" and "them" is commonly interpreted as "East" and "West" or as "totalitarianism" and "democracy." Viewed through the lens of God's kingdom, though, geographical and ideological distinctions are not the issue or the point of focus. That, in essence, is how the believers in China tend to view things. They are not concerned with categorizing the world or putting things into their "rightful" places.

When Abraham was in Canada in 2010, for instance, he was somewhat bewildered when a Caucasian lady asked him, "Which is better—communism or capitalism?" As a guest in the church, Abraham thought it would be impolite of him not to respond. The question, though, was not something that had crossed his mind before. "I don't know," he began to answer slowly. "I've only ever lived under communism. But it seems to me, whichever draws us closer to God would be better."

Much of Christendom is in the habit of shaking its head and lamenting the fact that there is little or no freedom of religion in China. *It isn't right that the faithful there are persecuted! It isn't just!* Notwithstanding the rightness or wrongness, however, the reality is that Chinese Christians in the Mainland do not spend much time deliberating this issue. Nor do they exert much energy complaining about it. It's just the way things are. They get on with life.

A case in point: the 200 or so Christians who were barred from leaving China to attend a global Christian conference in South Africa, the Third Lausanne Congress on World Evangelization, in 2010.[1] Some of the Christians were placed under house arrest; others had their passports confiscated; and still others were turned back at the airport boarding gates and sent home. But in whatever way the believers fell victim to this prohibition, including a couple of the leaders in this book, it was not cause for them to lament the lost opportunity to go to Cape Town or to march to Beijing to fight for their rights. Instead, many of them redirected their energies toward the doors that *were* open to them—namely, planning outreach events or missions trips to minority regions within the PRC.

The heritage of the house church is such that individuals who make a commitment to Christ instinctively know that they now have the responsibility to preach the gospel, regardless of how much or how little they know of the Bible; regardless of how long or how short a time they have been a believer. They know it's not an easy path they've chosen to walk. It's a serious life decision. And the urban church leaders in this book can be counted in here too. As such, their relationship with Jesus naturally becomes fully integrated into their everyday lives. In time, it becomes their identity, including the hard parts about Jesus' life, even His suffering.

基督教

Job and his wife became Christians in 2002. They gave up their plans to move to Australia and committed themselves to living in China. They would do their part to help China get saved. Yet the road was anything but smooth.

Both Job and his wife were well educated and successful in their careers. As university sweethearts, they were part of China's upwardly mobile, riding the wave of the new prosperity; and for all of their married life together they had been accustomed to enjoying the material and financial benefits of their times. But life with Jesus, they were discovering, was challenging everything they were, including their whole way of thinking.

It began with the qualms Job's wife began to have about her work. A qualified pediatrician, she had resigned her position as a doctor at a hospital a few years earlier to work for a pharmaceutical company. The market was opening up and her friends encouraged her to capitalize on the opportunities to make easy money. Her new job would only require her to promote the company's medicines. The more doctors who agreed to use them, the more money she would earn.

She had now been working for the same pharmaceutical company for three years, and she had flourished in the role. The work was so much easier than diagnosing problems with children, and it was less stressful. The hours were regular and she didn't have to work late night shifts at the hospital anymore. To top it all off, she was earning five times the amount of money she earned as a doctor. Her friends were right: It *was* easy money.

But one day a work colleague challenged her about the ethics of bribing doctors to use medicines and receiving kickbacks. "Aren't you a Christian now?" she was asked. "You shouldn't be doing this. You shouldn't be corrupt."

Such was the reputation of Christians in the new China.

Job and his wife had not expected this. Was the colleague right? Was bribery wrong? If it was, what should she do? Should she quit her job? It wasn't easy to get a job in China, especially a well-paying job. If she quit, they might not be able to provide their son with all the good things they were accustomed to. Surely God wouldn't want them to deprive their son of good things? Yet, they read it in the Bible: Jesus said there was a cost to following Him. Was this the price He was asking them to pay now?

In the days that followed, they weighed the pros and cons of her leaving the pharmaceutical company against what they were reading in the Bible. It was hard to know what to do. So many people in China did this. It was a generally accepted, normal business practice. Did this mean they were all corrupt?

While Job and his wife were deliberating the matter, Job heard of a Christian conference to be held in Hong Kong. It sounded like it might be good to help him and his wife grow in their faith; so he decided to register the two of them to attend. Maybe they would find an answer to their dilemma there. But when she applied for time off work to go to the conference, Job's wife couldn't get it. Her boss would not approve the leave.

Job was set on the two of them going to the conference. The more he thought about it the more he felt it was important for them to go. He realized that the conference would indeed help them in their faith, only a little quicker than he had anticipated and not quite in the way he would have expected. He asked his wife to think about resigning from the pharmaceutical company. He told her the Bible says that God provides. "So we'll trust Him to provide another job for you, and we'll trust Him to provide for our son," he said. She agreed, and that was the end of that.

基督教

In 2003, Job and his wife began a home group with a few friends. The fellowship was small—fewer than 20 members—in the first couple of years. In 2006, things took a turn, and the church began to grow in numbers. Job experienced one dramatic week in that pivotal year that would prove to be one of the markers of the breakthrough.

He had been invited to go to Chicago, Illinois, to share his testimony with some churches there. It was one of the first times that he had been asked to minister in the United States. His host had arranged for an older Chinese American man to accompany and assist him while he was stateside, since Job did not speak much English. This man happened to be a medical doctor. This older doctor's area of specialty was the heart and lungs, and his reputation was such that he had been invited to China on several occasions over the years to consult on the individual cases of various high government officials in Beijing.

During the time they were together in Chicago, the two doctors had many conversations and became friends. One day, the older man received news from his family that his younger sister, who was in her 70s, had been diagnosed with lung cancer. Her case was terminal. As a matter of course, he shared this with Job. Naturally, after some discussion, the two doctors wanted to examine her medical file and asked the family if they could see it. When the two friends had reviewed her X-ray, MRI and CT scans, along with all the other test results, they could see there had been no mistake; it was definitely cancer. Other than try to alleviate some of her pain and discomfort, there was nothing else, medically speaking, they could offer or do for her. They could only pray and hope for some divine intervention.

Job had been having trouble sleeping during the trip because of jetlag, and that night was no exception. As usual, his sleep was broken, and he found himself abruptly awake very early in the morning. When he looked at the clock it was 4:00 A.M. With the case of his friend's sister on his heart, he decided to spend some time in prayer for her instead of trying to get back to sleep. "I didn't get up out of my bed," he said. "I just prayed for his sister while lying there."

Several hours later, by the time the two doctors met at breakfast, Job felt sure that he had heard a clear word from God about the sister's situation during his prayer time. He decided to share it with his friend and said, "The Lord has assured me that He has healed your sister." This word brought grateful tears to the elder man's eyes, and they began to roll down his cheek. To him it was amazing. He was moved by God's love for him and by Job's sharing, because it confirmed exactly what he had heard during his own sleepless and prayerful night.

Later that day, after they finished their scheduled ministry, the two doctors shared about the older man's sister and her illness with the people of the church. They concluded by inviting the whole assembly to pray with them for her. Soon afterward, Job's trip was finished. He left the United States and flew back home to China.

A few days later, back in Wuhan, Job received a phone call from the older doctor in Chicago. The older man's sister had gone back to her doctors for another medical appointment. Upon re-examination they found absolutely no trace of the cancer in her body. She was healed! It was as if she had never contracted the disease. The doctors couldn't understand what happened. The results of her earlier tests clearly showed that there was cancer, but they couldn't explain why it was not there anymore.

Later in that same week, two women in Job's church approached the doctor separately to tell him that they had been diagnosed with cancer. The women had each heard through the grapevine that a Chinese American lady had recently been healed of the disease. If God could heal cancer in the United States, they asked Job, could He do the same in China? Both of the ladies were fairly new Christians, and in one of them, the cancer had already metastasized.

Unbeknownst to the women, the question turned out to be a subconscious challenge to Job. While he had no doubt that God loved him and that Jesus Christ was alive in him, there was still a small, niggling part of him that wondered, like many others in his country, if Christianity was not in actuality a foreign religion.

So when the two women posed their question, he felt it acutely. *Would God really heal here in the People's Republic too?* He wanted to know, and he was definitely up for this test of faith.

Job called the church fellowship together, and he was bold when he told the women in front of the people gathered there that God could heal them. He then proceeded to share the testimony of this Chinese American lady, for those who hadn't yet heard, of how she had just been healed of cancer by the Lord only days before; then he invited the whole group to come forward and lay hands on their two sisters. Fifteen people came together in faith to encircle them, and they all prayed in agreement with Job.

Over the next few days, Job accompanied both of the ladies to their medical appointments, which were at two of the top hospitals in the city. As with the sister in Chicago, they each underwent reexamination by their doctors, and in both cases it was found that, incredibly, the cancer cells were no longer present in either of the two women from his church! They, too, had been healed!

Job is still blown away when he recalls those events. "In one week, I experienced three miracles! If you ask me as a doctor and as a professor of medicine how I explain this, well, I don't explain it! I can't! I just praise and worship God!" He sat in awed silence for a short while, then concluded, "God *is* in the business of healing. We doctors and all our medicines and science—we're all just tools in His hands. Ultimately, the power and authority to heal and perform miracles are His."

Job went on to state that he firmly believes that signs and wonders should not be viewed as a thing of the past or as only belonging to the Early Church. He says they are "business as usual" with Jesus, and they are certainly meant for today's Church.

Today, the fellowship group has come into its own as a full-fledged church with roughly 300 members. It is comprised mainly of medical professionals, academics and businesspeople from the marketplace; multiple services run over the weekend, including a young-adults meeting on Saturday and family services on Sunday. Job is part of the pastoral team; he shares preaching and counseling responsibilities with another pastor, while his wife is in charge of the Sunday School and helps out with the ushering.

The church has not gone unnoticed by local officials, and Job has always endeavored to be open and straightforward with them. He has also tried to hear them out and understand their point of view. Relations have been cordial, but the church is still regularly invited or urged to register with the government. When this happens, Job understands that the officials are just doing their job.

As far as Job is concerned, the two main stumbling blocks to the TSPM are, first, its emphasis on justification by love and works, as opposed to faith; and second, the fact that evangelizing and missions are never encouraged or even mentioned. Yet, Job firmly believes that caring about your neighbor or community is an imperative for the Church. It is an integral part of bringing social justice to the place that the Church is located.

"Christians are called to be light in the darkness, a city on a hill, so they will be noticed," he says. "What it comes down to is that we should be a model of social responsibility and, as such, there should be some thought and deliberateness given to our actions to reach out in this way." He recognizes, however, that the house church has traditionally been somewhat shy in this because the natural tendency developed after years of persecution is to protect and hide oneself from official eyes. It is not easy to break a habit or behavior that has been an integral part of who you are.

In addition, the comparative freedom the unregistered churches have had to assemble in the last 20 years has meant that their focus has tended to stay primarily on themselves rather than on those outside the church. After all, it's not every day they are actually able to set their own goals and implement their own plans for church growth and development; it's not often they find themselves left so unobstructed in their efforts. Usually they are too busy just trying to stay afloat and survive.

Job's church, however, has embarked on the path to live and demonstrate social responsibility. One way they are doing this is by reaching out to their community through a food bank. This is a new concept in China, and theirs is the first in their city and, indeed, the country. At its grand opening in 2010, despite initial efforts to keep the event low key, local officials ended up attending, and media were also present to provide news coverage. There was even a report that aired on national TV.

This inaugural food bank was established in Wuhan, the largest city in central China by population, with roughly a million and a half more people than New York. The city is a major transportation hub and educational center and, historically, is the place where Dr. Sun Yat Sen's followers launched an uprising that led to the downfall of the Qing Dynasty and the founding of the Republic of China in 1911.

The idea for the food bank was inspired by a trip overseas the previous year. Job was visiting a church in the United States that happened to run a food bank in their community, and the work profoundly impressed him. After discussing and researching the operation with the American organizers, he decided a food bank would be both beneficial and workable in China.

The local government in Wuhan was favorable toward the idea and invited Job and his church to visit poor families in specific areas of the city, which they had identified, to help them interview and gain a better understanding of the social services they needed beyond the food bank. As a result, these visits became a further extension of the compassion ministry his church was already running among the elderly and poor in their own neighborhood, which included preparing and distributing care packages that contained items like food hampers and blankets, depending on the season.

At the present time, the food bank relies on the help of volunteers and the good will of corporate and individual sponsors. While many volunteers do come from the church, the intent is to keep the two operations separate and independent from each other.

In running the center, Job tries to be transparent in his relations with the local officials. When the food bank creates marketing plans or advertisements, for example, he generally likes to provide the local government with advance notice so they will know what's in the pipeline, thus giving them reassurance that the efforts continue for the holistic development of the community. It seems to be working out well.

"So far," says Job, "the government is giving us their support. The biggest blessing, though, is not that, or even that poor people are being helped. It's actually the people who are serving, those who volunteer to serve, who receive the greatest blessing." Job pauses to collect his thoughts. "People in the area know the food bank was started by Christians. They like the fact that we brought something good into their community. They don't want us to leave. That's a true blessing."

In the longer term the vision is to grow the capacity of the food bank and create more outlets in different parts of the city for the convenience of the needy.

基督教

While able to enjoy amicable relations with local officials, Job has not always experienced smooth sailing at the national level—but not for want of trying. He continues to make an honest effort to build relationships with officials at all levels as opportunities come up.

In recent years, consistent with the closer monitoring of unregistered churches and the slightly more restrictive climate, Job has occasionally popped up on the federal-level radar. This has resulted in a few episodes of harassment, which has generally taken the form of detainment or delay at immigration just as he is about to board a plane, and sporadic following by the police. (On one occasion, he was refused permission to board an international flight and was subsequently sent home.) This kind of official attention is unwanted, of course, but Job is undeterred. He puts his head down, his shoulder to the wheel and keeps working while he can to build up the Church and community around him.

"Persecution and pressure," says Job, "are times of shaking. Some parts fall away in a shaking. But for those who stay, they are the core of the Church. That testimony is very powerful, especially if you're a leader, because it has an effect on what others will do in the future, if they will stay standing too."

"That type of believer is rare," adds Abraham. The pastor from Shanghai surmises that in an average church, less than 5 percent of the people would be so firmly committed. "It's inevitable that some will leave when there is persecution," he continues, "and as a leader, unfortunately, I will lose many friends." He speaks from recent experience.

After further thought, Abraham says, "It's not easy to know what to do when you're facing pressure or undergoing persecution. One person tells you to be bold and strong, to stand firm on principle. Another thinks negotiating would be the better route—why not give up a little control or independence to keep the church going? Fewer people would suffer that way. Who's to say which way is better?"

Paul speaks up and says, "I think only Christians in China can really understand how hard it is to make this kind of decision." The pastor from Xiamen is talking about the pressure for churches to register with the government. The vehicle through which churches are supposed to register is the Three Self Patriotic Movement, which was established in 1951 and promoted the "values" that churches should be self-governing, self-supporting and self-propagating. While some churches joined, others did not. It soon came to light, however, that those who were not registered were being reported to officials by some of those that had. "That is where the mistrust between the house church and the Three Self church all began," Paul says, "and it's been hard to break, especially when people see that so many Christians have been imprisoned and have suffered for their faith over the years."

The reputation of the Three Self Patriotic Movement has taken such a beating that officials decided to form the China Christian Council (CCC) in 1980, to be an umbrella organization over the Protestant churches in the country. As part of its purview, the CCC deviates from the traditional "self" values of the TSPM in that it also seeks to develop friendly relations with churches abroad. In practice, the CCC is the governing body in China that is responsible for resolving theological issues, while the TSPM is the administrator. As such, the TSPM remains the sole official registration vehicle for churches today.

"There are some pastors in the Three Self Patriotic Movement who have honorable and sincere intentions," says Paul. "Some of them think it's easier to preach the gospel if they have the government's covering. You can also see that in some cities there are large congregations in the Three Self church. But when you talk to the people there, their emphasis is mostly on doing good works. Maybe I'm wrong, but there doesn't seem to be much spiritual depth beyond that."

Paul goes on to talk about a senior pastor of a TSPM church that he knows. This pastor heads the church's pastoral team, which is comprised of a total of three people, including him. Traditionally, TSPM churches do not involve laypeople in their ministries, so the tiny team is run off their feet because they alone are responsible for tending to the needs of their congregation, which consists of 3,500 people. "How can that many people be pastored by so few?" Paul asks. "Even if you have the heart and will to serve God in this capacity, there's only so much a person can do in one day."

Why don't they expand the team and get more pastors?

"To be a pastor in the Three Self church," Paul explains, "you need the endorsement of the government. There are actually a lot of graduates from Bible seminaries, even from Three Self schools. But if they aren't chosen or elected by the officials to be a pastor in the Three Self church, they won't be appointed to serve in a church." There is a moment of grim silence as Paul reflects further on this, then concludes, "It's not right. It's not right that a non-believing body should have any influence in the relationship between the Church and God."

Note

1. Staff Reporter, "Beijing Bars Churches from Conference," *South China Morning Post* (October 16, 2010).

4

An NGO Pioneer

"Let's go at once to take the land," [Caleb] said.
"We can certainly conquer it!"

NUMBERS 13:30

CALEB WAS AWAY FROM HOME when it happened. He was in Yunnan province, preparing his presentations and materials for a conference he was scheduled to speak at on how to run social welfare and development programs in the Mainland. His was a rare entity in the Chinese Christian community—a bona fide nongovernmental organization (NGO) in the PRC, complete with government approval and certification. Partway through the afternoon, though, he got a phone call.

"It's canceled."

"It's canceled?"

"The conference. We're canceling it."

"What? Why? Why are you canceling?" Caleb was aghast. How could this be happening? He had spent days, weeks preparing for this. Establishing schools for disabled children, poverty relief for minority orphans, and care for lepers had been a hard slog over the past 16 years, but they were his passion and represented his life's work. He took pride in every opportunity to share his experience with others who were aspiring to do as he was.

"There's been an earthquake. Turn on your TV," the organizer of the conference said.

Caleb turned it on. As the scenes of rubble and disaster filled the screen, he sank back on the hotel bed in shock. It was May 12, 2008, and the Great Sichuan Earthquake had just happened. With a magnitude that measured 7.9 on the Richter scale and a duration of about two minutes, the quake struck at 2:28 PM and could be felt as far away in the country as Beijing and Shanghai. The epicenter was in the county of Wenchuan, 80 kilometers from his home city of Chengdu.

Caleb tried to call home on his mobile. He needed to find out where his wife and son were. But he couldn't get through. He tried again, entreating his wife to answer the phone. Still there was no answer. A notice flashed across the TV screen that mobile networks were inoperable because of the quake. He went down to the lobby to place a call on the hotel's landline. It took several more attempts before an anxious Caleb finally managed to connect.

After checking on his family and finding them all accounted for, he told his wife to begin mobilizing their network of house churches in the province to send volunteers to help with the disaster relief while he traveled home. A day and a half later, Caleb managed to make his way back home to Chengdu, just in time to join the several hundred Christian volunteers his wife had assembled, including more than 20 doctors.

Originally, they, as a team, were assigned to go to Beichuan, which turned out to be one of the hardest hit areas with most of its buildings destroyed and about half of its 20,000 population killed. (Officially, as of July 2008, there were overall totals of 69,197 dead, 374,176 injured and more than 18,000 missing from the earthquake.) But because Premier Wen Jiabao was visiting when they arrived, they were redirected to Anxian, a neighboring area. There they teamed up with PLA soldiers and experienced mountaineers and were assigned to the search and rescue of survivors from the numerous landslides triggered by the quake.

The work proved to be slow and arduous. The terrain was mountainous, and some villages had been completely cut off by the landslides. Reaching them proved to be a herculean task. There was extensive damage to many roads, often rendering them impassable and making transport by foot the only option. But even that was not always possible. In some cases, Caleb and his team found themselves lowering ropes down slopes to help people climb their way out of the valleys.

On another occasion, because vehicles couldn't get in or out of the area, the helpers formed a long human chain. One by one the injured were carried and passed from one set of arms to another, from one person to the next until they were clear of the danger zone.

Beyond the sore, aching limbs and bleeding hands, the real trauma that all the relief workers suffered was seeing the extent of the human loss firsthand. "The smell of death was so strong," says Caleb. "Job and his team gave out so many masks. At first the dead were buried one by one. But later, because there were so many bodies, they had to spray disinfectant to prevent disease, and dig mass graves."

Death was literally all around, Caleb recalls. "When people are exposed to that day after day, hour after hour, it's completely overwhelming. Nobody could sleep well at night. Nobody could get the images out of their minds, not even the soldiers."

基督教

Even before the earthquake, Job already had it on his heart to develop a compassion ministry that focused on meeting needs through the development of social services and the provision of disaster relief.

Job saw that the churches in China were growing in number and he believed they should be proactive to help in everyday situations and to bring aid in times of catastrophe.

"A lot of churches have no problem accepting the Great Commission," he says, "and so they emphasize personal salvation. But they haven't been as effective in carrying out the Great Commandment. Very little thought has been given toward how to show true love to our neighbor, to our community, to developing ministries that demonstrate this. We need to figure out a way to do this." The doctor goes on to state his belief that if they can do that, the government would not shun help from the churches, especially if their ministries were social welfare programs that could benefit local communities. They might even appreciate it.

The final seeds of his conviction had been sown in early 2008, in advance of the Chinese New Year. The most important and anticipated traditional holiday in the PRC, this annual celebration is commonly referred to as Spring Festival by the locals, although that year, in accordance with the lunar calendar, it fell in the bitter cold month of February. It was a time that most of the country ended up experiencing its harshest winter in 50 years.

Ahead of the heavy, busy holiday travel season, at the end of January, severe snow storms and freezing temperatures in the southern and central regions caused considerable damage, power outages and transportation disruptions for thousands of people. Among other problems, tens of thousands of travelers were stranded in railway stations in the south of the country and thousands of flights were canceled at various airports, ratcheting up the number of helpless people by thousands more. The humanitarian need that winter had been very real indeed. In the end, more than 100 people died as a result of the storms. It was then that Job knew he should begin planning and preparations for future emergencies, sooner rather than later.

When the earthquake struck on May 12, Job and Abraham were quick to mobilize a small squad of Christians from their churches to help the relief efforts. While their churches continued to gather more helpers, equipment and money, Job, Abraham and their little group were among the earliest to arrive on the scene, along with the PLA and government officials. Believers also came from many other churches, including Caleb's and Paul's, and they all united under one banner as the "China ActionLove Volunteers Association." All told, more than 3,000 Christians came from around the country to help in Sichuan. It was a unified effort that impressed the government, and the China ActionLove Volunteers Association was later acknowledged and honored for their endeavors by President Hu Jintao at a special banquet for charities and NGOs in Beijing.

The earthquake proved to be an excellent starting point for the compassion ministry, and an ongoing and invaluable education for Job. It was the place to begin learning about and practicing how to provide disaster relief; and later, when the rebuilding phase began, how to develop NGO and social service programs.

The foreign aid agencies and other relief helpers have long since left the stricken zone, but Job's team has remained. Today they are building kindergartens and small community centers in the area. The community centers, which constitute the main thrust of their projects, are being constructed across the needy counties. Each one provides basic medical clinic care, counseling services, a library and an activity room. Through the connections made at the centers, Job's team matches up churches in the nearby areas to orphans, the elderly and other needy people so that they can follow up accordingly. In the two years after the earthquake, Job's team managed to construct 15 community centers, each of which serves 4,000 to 6,000 people.

Beyond meeting immediate practical needs in the region, the community centers are a unifying platform from which many churches, including those from overseas, are able to reach out to the local communities who suffered loss and damage from the earthquake. To date, more than 300 churches have been involved in caring for the people of Sichuan through these centers. At the same time, the centers have encouraged house churches in the area to look beyond their own walls—to begin to emerge from a protective shell that was induced by years of persecution.

The community centers are a place where people can learn practical skills, such as first aid or outdoor survival techniques. They are also a place where believers are encouraged to learn more about their faith—what they believe in and why. They embrace a holistic approach to caring for the community, and even those who come for visits from overseas have had life-changing experiences. A Chinese church in Chicago, for example, sent some teams for short spells to help out at the community centers. The pastor of the church reported back to Job that his fellowship has since seen transformation back in the Windy City as a result of their people coming to Sichuan. The congregation has grown in size, as have the offerings, and the prayer life of the members has changed dramatically. The pastor was so encouraged by what he saw.

Closer to home, Job tells of a senior man who was paralyzed. This man had been neglected in his village for 20 years; no one in his family or the neighborhood ever came to visit him. He was all but forgotten. But one day, Job's team discovered him, and in so doing, they undertook to care for him daily by cooking meals and helping him to bathe. After several days, some of the villagers began to notice that the man was receiving attention. It aroused their curiosity, and they learned that Job's team was diligently caring for their disabled neighbor. Eventually, this prompted a change in their own attitude and behavior toward the man, and the local people were no longer oblivious to his existence or condition. Some of them even began helping him too.

At first, churches in the nearby area were skeptical about the goals of the community centers and the training that was provided through them. Yet, many have now seen that a proactive approach to caring for their neighborhood can make a difference. They've also seen how it has helped to create a more disciplined and mature attitude in their own members. It is one small step toward instilling life-affirming values in a rapidly changing society that has too often become consumed by the pursuit of money and material things.

基督教

Caleb is an entrepreneur, a self-made millionaire, in *renminbi* terms. He began his own pharmaceutical company in 1988 and was fortunate to strike it rich within a couple of years. By the early 1990s, he was on the lookout for new investment opportunities. The thin, sprightly, smiley man at first thought that he might open a private kindergarten to cater to the children of China's growing number of wealthy elite. But then he saw a child in a wheelchair, and that changed his whole outlook.

"It's unusual to see disabled children on the street in China," says Caleb, remembering his walk that day. "They're usually viewed as an embarrassment to the family, and so they're hidden away."

Yet, this child was sitting there outside, in plain sight of everyone passing by. He smiled at Caleb. Caleb's heart melted, and the entrepreneur had a new inspiration. He would set up a home and a school for disabled children.

The first of his schools for the disabled was established in 1993. Caleb invested more than US$100,000 into the facility, and within a couple of years there were more than 30 disabled children living there. The Holy Love School was registered as a private business even though the intention and purpose were to provide aid and educational services for disabled kids. As such the student fees were nominal. In effect, it was a not-for-profit operation. This structure may seem strange to onlookers in the West, but at the time, the laws in China were not conducive to forming nonprofit organizations. To this day, the setting of official policy in the PRC and lawmaking in general are not able to keep pace with the reality on the ground, and it continues to play catch-up.

The philanthropy and nonprofit sector is a prime example. One of the advantages of forming a private foundation is that there will be tax breaks, because the reasons for its existence and work are not for profit—at least this is the understanding in North America. In China, however, the private foundation is still subject to tax on capital gains. By definition, an NGO operates as an independent organization, free from government intervention, so far as those in the West understand it. Yet, in order to legally obtain NGO status in China, the entity must have a sponsor or supervisor from a government department or authorized government organization—and this is where the real challenge lies. This is a major reason why many organizations that do NGO work in China are registered as corporations or not registered at all. More often than not, they are unable to meet the government-sponsor requirement. According to the Ministry of Civil Affairs, however, new rules are expected to be issued by the end of 2013 to make the registration process for many NGOs easier.[1] Nevertheless, the revised regulations will exclude those organizations considered political or religious.[2]

Caleb achieved charitable status for the Holy Love Foundation in November 1994. The foundation was unique, because China, at that time, did not have the custom of creating private organizations in order to help society. In a socialist state, that is supposed to be the government's job. Moreover, the concept of his organization—to help the disabled—was not an area of high priority or importance for the government and was not well received by authorizing officials. The Education Commission, for instance, initially said that disabled children did not concern them and that they would therefore not support his application for the school.

The disabled, as viewed in traditional Chinese culture, are a cause of shame and therefore should not be visible. If they are not visible, so the official thinking usually goes, what would be the point in investing efforts and money toward helping them? The odds of Caleb's foundation achieving charitable status were against him, at the time; but ultimately, through much perseverance and prayer, the Holy Love Foundation was established as a genuine homegrown NGO. This feat came long before philanthropy, volunteering, giving back and making donations became the latest trend in the PRC.

In the past 30 years, with its gradual opening, the country's market has increasingly adopted characteristics and ideas found in developed economies, including the beginnings of a nonprofit sector. According to Xinhua, the Chinese news agency, the nation has seen "rapid growth" in the number of private charitable foundations since 2007, and expectations are that there will be a "charity boom over the next 10 to 20 years."[3]

The underlying motivation behind Caleb's foundation is found in Jesus' words recorded in Mark 12:30-31, where He tells believers to love the Lord with all your heart and with all your soul and mind, and to love your neighbor as yourself. It is the poor, the weak and the disadvantaged who are impressed on Caleb, who was born into a Christian family; and today a large portion of his foundation's work is directed toward providing educational facilities and poverty relief for the ethnic minority peoples in the country. Presently, that involves serving those in Sichuan, Yunnan and Guizhou provinces.

Officially, China has 55 ethnic minority groups. Combined, they comprise less than 10 percent of the country's total population. Yunnan and Guizhou, in particular, are known for having large numbers of minorities, with 25 and 49 different people groups living in those provinces respectively. Caleb's long-term vision is to reach out to every one of the minority groups in the country.

The Holy Love Foundation also provides care and residential facilities for lepers in a handful of villages in Liangshan, an autonomous region for the Yi tribe in Sichuan. Overall, there are about 600 leper colonies and 20,000 lepers in the PRC. The three provinces the Holy Love Foundation works in happen to contain areas where the disease is mostly found in China, though it is also found in other parts of the country. Until 1987, the central government's policy was to isolate those with leprosy, and the colonies tended to be located in remote areas that were difficult to access, such as mountainous regions. Though leprosy is treatable, in keeping with the custom of the land, the practice was to hide those who did not appear to be "normal" or who had a visible disability, for they were thought to be a source of shame. The heart of the Holy Love founder is to help these people to know that they are loved and accepted just the way they are.

Another minority that Caleb serves are the Zang, more commonly known in the West as the Tibetans. According to the 2000 census figures, there are a total of 5.4 million Tibetans living in China. This makes them the country's tenth largest minority group. Roughly half of the Zang live in the Tibet Autonomous Region, while the other half can be found in neighboring provinces, including Qinghai, Sichuan, Gansu and Yunnan.

With the Sichuan quake, and the 2010 Yushu earthquake in Qinghai, Caleb's tent in recent years has increasingly been stretched. The Yushu quake, in particular, has opened new doors for him to serve the Tibetan people. One of the first projects he established there was a medical clinic. Donations of medical supplies and food have come from local and international sources, including from churches. The immediate objective was to help the victims heal from their physical and emotional wounds, and to care for the Buddhist monks, some of whom refused to return to live in their temples after the quake because they feared the potential devastation from aftershocks. Instead, they asked if they could receive aid from Caleb and his team. This has led to opportunities for him to evangelize a number of them.

"The important thing is to build relationships with them," says Caleb. "We want those relationships to be as good as possible. We want to help them and build their trust. If they suggest people for us to help, for instance, we will follow up on them. We try to help in whatever way we can."

Caleb tells a story about one particular monk in the region, whose mother happens to be handicapped. This woman was in need of a wheelchair and asked Caleb's team if they could provide her with one. After considering their budget and resources, however, the team said no to her request. Later, when Caleb learned of their decision, he asked them why they had declined to help her. Their answer? The monk should take care of his own mother. They said he is obviously wealthy—you can see it in the big car he drives! He would have no problem affording the cost of buying a wheelchair. He could also easily manage the cost of hiring someone to take care of her, but he does not do it.

Caleb understood why they felt and acted the way they did, but the more he thought about it, the more he did not have peace inside. He felt like God was prompting him to intervene. In the end, he overrode their decision. He found a wheelchair in Chengdu and had it sent to the woman. His team did not understand why their leader did this.

"It's precisely because the monk has money and does not choose to care for his mother that we should do it," Caleb patiently explained to them. "People will see that it's the Christians who have taken care of his mother, not the son or the Buddhist leader, as would normally be expected. Don't you see? This is an opportunity for us to demonstrate the love of Jesus."

Slowly, a few of the monks in the region are beginning to come to Christ, and it is encouraging for Caleb to see. But he is not the type to be content with just a few and to sit back on his laurels. Ever on the lookout for lost sheep, he has already identified more people to reach out to. Since the Yushu quake, for instance, the doors have continued to open for him, one of which led to a certain Tibetan monk in the region who has been bedridden for the past three years. Caleb explains that this monk used to be very flamboyant and charismatic before he fell ill, but now no one cares for him. He has basically been forgotten. When the Holy Love leader learned of his existence, he went to visit him at his home. The place was squalid and full of flies, but it didn't discourage Caleb from offering love, hope and help.

The monk was grateful for the succor, and since then, Caleb and his team have faithfully come to help him with food, to tidy the house a bit, to run some errands and to provide friendly companionship. Caleb believes that after the monk comes to know Christ, his testimony will have a large influence on many people in the area because of his past reputation. Caleb is also praying for the monk to walk again. "And I believe that we will see this miracle happen," he says with a smile.

When he first went to help with the relief effort of the Sichuan earthquake, Caleb's original intent was to go for the sake of the children. The scale of the devastation he saw, though, forced him to broaden his vision. "There were just too many people who had so many needs," he said. He simply felt that they could not be ignored.

基督教

"The goal is that the skills taught will be easily transferable to other situations and places," says Job. The doctor is talking about the training courses run out of the community centers in Sichuan. "Eventually, we would like them to be carried beyond the local community into other regions, provinces and even nations. When young people attend a course, we hope they will be inspired for life. They're not just going to gain some practical skills. Through the fellowship and team situations, directly or indirectly, they're going to be exposed to godly values, to biblical principles, and learn to become socially responsible people of character. We hope their vision of the world will be expanded. Maybe one day they'll even want to go out to the mission field themselves."

On top of this, Job has devised a six-lesson course specifically geared toward churches on how to apply both the Great Commission and the Great Commandment at the same time. Its rollout is still in the early stages, and the course, no doubt, will be further refined over time; but he has already taught it in several different cities, and it has been favorably received not only by the churches but by some government officials as well. There are even some in the Religious Affairs Bureau who have asked for his materials.

"I believe the next step for the Church in China as a whole, whether rural, urban or Three Self," says Job with conviction, "is to learn how to actually touch the community with the love and power of the gospel." Despite the growth of Christianity in the country to date, the doctor believes the Church is still not doing this effectively. That growth, he says, was due more to a *kairos* period, a special window of time when God, in His grace, allowed people to find Him because they were so hungry.

"The Bible says that when you knock, the door will be opened to you; when you seek, you will find; and when you ask, it will be given to you. But [the churches] are all becoming more established now—with resources, finances and manpower multiplying. How can we use these more effectively to touch our communities with the love of Christ? We need to learn how to do that."

It's a gradual process to build up people to the point that they are both willing *and* able to handle being sent to the nations. Ruth echoes this: "It's about taking it step by step, and building true character takes time and patience. Not only should our missionaries be learning about the Bible and God, but they should also be learning practical skills to sustain their livelihoods and learn how to do what they do better." She pauses a moment to reflect on what she's seen thus far. "A lot of young people were sent out already. They were eager and willing. They were bold and courageous. But the truth is that they couldn't make it. They had unrealistic expectations, and so did their sending churches. As a result, the survival rate in the field was low because they didn't have viable skills to support themselves over the long term."

Ruth concludes, "You can't rush the growth of fruit, and it was wrong to expect a large harvest when they were first sent out. Instead, we should be encouraging them to focus on building relationships with local people, to live among them, eat with them and talk with them. Eventually, out of that will come ministry opportunities and fruit. We need to learn from what has already happened and not make the same mistakes again."

While there is no doubt that progress has been made on Job's front, the overall work is still in its infancy. Job admits that he is still learning the ropes in terms of providing beneficial social services and running a charitable organization.

One of the challenges he faces, for instance, is how to prioritize projects. The community centers have triggered a growing number of requests for help in other areas, even though his plate is already more than full. The needs are so great, but the resources are limited. To begin with, the centers need more volunteers, which then leads to the necessity for more trainers and better-quality training. But it is difficult to find a sufficient number of qualified trainers and materials within a country that is still in the midst of its development. Importing that help from abroad brings an additional set of challenges—among which language and cultural barriers are just the beginning.

Meeting the financial needs of the various projects is another hurdle. As Job says, "It's a faith lesson." And what a lesson it is. Although he has led a church for many years now, he says he's never experienced such a hard test as running an NGO operation like this. The operational budget is considerably larger than that for his church, up to RMB200,000 per month. At times, they have had as little as RMB200 in the bank to pay the bills.

"All you can do in that situation," says Job, "is pray. I'm not a person who likes to ask for anything, and I don't think I'm very good at it. But God provides! Every month I don't know where the money is going to come from, but God provides."

Job believes that registering with the government as an NGO would make the overall operation smoother and easier in terms of recruiting helpers and fundraising, and this is the direction he is aiming to move these community projects toward. In the long term, similar to Ruth's vision to envelop business in the cause for missions, Job hopes that the churches in China will learn to utilize compassion ministries on the same front.

"Even though we lacked experience coming into this, God has been faithful," says Job. "There have been so many lessons learned already, but God gives us what we need. He has already sent a lot of people—many angels and experts—to help us!"

As another example of the "angels" God has sent along his journey, Job tells the astounding story of how his church recently received favor and finances to help them purchase a new place for their meetings. "For me," the doctor begins, "miraculous healings, deliverances, setting people free from fear and bondage or reconciling broken relationships—whether husbands and wives, fathers and sons, or mothers and daughters—these are normal, regular occurrences in our church. We pray and speak the Word of truth, and God answers through the power of the Holy Spirit. That's the way it's supposed to be, isn't it?" There is a childlike simplicity in the man's faith as he asks this question. "But recently, we received permission to buy an entire floor of a commercial building in the central business district—now *that* is a miracle! The landlord was actually willing to sell it to us knowing that we are a church."

The atmosphere in the country has at times been somewhat restrictive toward Christian activities, and the property in question is located in the prime downtown area of Wuhan. The second miracle, Job says, is that while real estate prices have done nothing but skyrocket in China in recent years, the owner of the building was extremely favorable toward them, agreeing to sell it to them at a reduced rate. "It is almost unbelievable," Job says again with wonder. "And then you have to realize that we are a small congregation. We are a fairly young congregation; but within two weeks we were able to raise more than US$1.5 million to pay for the building. Now *that* is totally incredible. You are talking about people whose salaries get up to only RMB5,000 [about US$800] per month."

Job goes on to explain how there is no formal membership system in his church, but still the people were moved by the Holy Spirit to give toward this building project, and they were so generous. Renovations and other preparations for the new premises are currently underway, and some of the expertise and donations have come from unexpected places, namely from outside of the church. "We are so blessed," he says. "We are enjoying the favor of God and also the favor of man here—the neighbors, the community and even the authorities."

Yet, the road is long, and sometimes he needs encouragement. When that happens, the doctor returns to visit the man who first pointed him to Jesus: the American missionary who came to help save China.

Shortly after Job became a Christian, he decided to visit the missionary at his home. But the man was not there. His wife was home, however, and she invited the doctor in. Job was surprised that she knew who he was. The wife said the whole family knew of him—her husband, herself and their daughters. She explained to Job that her husband had died the year before, the victim of a tragic stabbing in Wuhan. Then she pulled out a photo album and showed Job a picture of her daughter who had visited his office with the injured hand. When her daughter and her husband had returned home from Job's office that pivotal day, they had removed the bandage and photographed the stitches. That very same night, their entire family began to pray for the doctor who had sewn these stitches—that he would come to know Jesus Christ. Job was moved to his core. It was at that point, he says, that he began to know that God hears and answers prayers.

The missionary was laid to rest at a cemetery in Wuhan, and Job now visits him there. "I do get a lot of encouragement when I'm there," the doctor says, "just thinking about how this man came from overseas because China needs salvation, and that his whole family prayed for me. They gave up their life in America to be here for us. If it were not for his example, I wouldn't have stayed in China. I would have moved to Australia."

Notes
1. He Dan, "New Rules for NGOs to Improve Operations," *China Daily* (April 17, 2013).
2. David Cohen, "Xi Jinping's Great Society," *The Diplomat* (April 25, 2013).
3. An, "Charity in China Expected to Boom as Private Charity Foundations Emerge," *Xinhua* (November 3, 2010).

5

Persecution and Suffering

*[The king] called out in anguish, "Daniel, servant of the living
God! Was your God, whom you serve so faithfully,
able to rescue you from the lions?"
Daniel answered, "Long live the king! My God sent his angel to
shut the lions' mouths so that they would not hurt me,
for I have been found innocent in his sight."*

DANIEL 6:20-22

"SUFFERING IS GOD'S PLAN." There was no drama in Daniel's voice as he said this, no heightened emotion. He said it plainly, his eyes focused ahead and his face framed by his rice bowl haircut. Daniel went on to tell the story of how one of his church elders was arrested and then beaten during an interrogation session. Interrogation, as those in China know, is part of the investigative process of a crime, and the beating the elder received was so severe, he passed out.

Emotion now began to stir in Daniel's voice as he related the next part. "Later, back in his prison cell, he told God that he couldn't bear it anymore. He was bowed before the Lord in prayer, and while on his knees, he saw a vision of Jesus nailed to the cross. He saw the precious blood flowing down from His wounds. And then he knew. He knew that Jesus suffered for him too." Daniel began to sing the song his church elder sang. "The Lord remembers His people, and there is nothing to fear. The Lord remembers His people. There is nothing to fear."

It's a lesson that Daniel has taken to heart. He may not have experienced persecution to the same degree as that of his elder; nevertheless, he has borne his share of hardships. He was arrested in 1997—the year Hong Kong was returned by the British to Chinese sovereignty—just as he had returned from a business trip to Wenzhou, his home city. Officials at the time were fearful that there would be some kind of pact or treaty made between churches in the former British colony and the port city of Zhejiang province. Hence the decision was made in the Mainland to clamp down on all known Christian activities—and consequently, the leaders—in the Wenzhou area. Daniel was detained in a city jail for one month on no specified charge—at least he was never informed of the charge.

"The thing that's hard," his wife interjects, "is that you don't know what's going on." While he was imprisoned, she was not allowed to visit him, not even once. When she asked, she was never given an answer as to what her husband's crime was. All she was told was that he would be in jail for a year. Yet, he was released after a month.

In the year 2000, local officials instituted another crackdown in the area. This time, it was a broader campaign against "feudal superstition." The targets of the campaign were Christian churches and Buddhist and Daoist temples and shrines. The original dictate stipulated that Christians, Buddhists and Daoists had to tear down their "illegal" structures—in other words, those that were not registered with the government. When they did not, which is hardly surprising, the authorities sent demolition teams with explosives around the city to blow up the buildings.

With their own church facing the threat of destruction, Daniel and his wife joined with their fellow members to pray about what they should do when the officials and demolition teams came knocking at their door. Through divine guidance and wisdom, they appointed a small group of a few leaders, including Daniel, to go and reason with the government officials.

In making their case to the officials, the church leaders calmly and respectfully cited the words of the Chinese constitution, which guarantees the right of citizens to enjoy freedom of religious belief. The church leaders said that the decree to demolish churches was therefore unconstitutional, because it infringed on their freedom to believe. Furthermore, they said, children are also protected under the constitution as citizens of the People's Republic, so they, too, are entitled to the same freedom. (Officials had counter-argued that the church was proselytizing people under the age of 18, which was illegal.)

The discussions between the church leaders and officials went on for hours and hours. The officials finally said they would need to take more time to consider the points, and sent the Christians home. When the church leaders returned to the government offices at the appointed date and time to resume the dialogue, they were left waiting in the lobby for more than two hours. No one from the government's side showed up. In the end, they departed, never having had the chance to meet the officials and finish making their case—but then neither was their church demolished.

Daniel laughs as he remembers this. "God is working among us," he says.

基督教

Wenzhou, of course, is renowned among believers in the Mainland as the Jerusalem of China for its considerable population of Christians. The largest port city in the south of the province, Wenzhou experienced a surge in its number of believers in the years following 1976, the end of the Cultural Revolution. The Wenzhou Christians are a major reason that Zhejiang has the highest proportion of believers in the country, with some estimates for the province reaching as high as 18.5 percent of its population.[1]

In 2010, that percentage amounted to more than 9 million Christians in the province. And, as evidenced by the 2000 campaign to demolish the abundant number of unregistered religious buildings in Wenzhou, it is plain to see that Christianity is alive and well in the city. There are, in fact, believers in Wenzhou who think that the original dictate to destroy the buildings had to come from higher up, as opposed to originating in local government offices, because it is common knowledge in the area that many officials at the municipal level are also Christians.

Until the late 1970s and early 1980s, when Deng Xiaoping instituted his economic reforms, there had been very little state investment in Wenzhou. The place, in short, was just a poor rural area. Situated on the coast in hilly terrain, across from Taiwan, agriculture was minimal and urban development was not high on the priority list. The logic of the time dictated that if the rebel province were to attack the Mainland, Wenzhou would be one of the first targets. As a result, the people of Wenzhou grew accustomed to fending for themselves, beginning first by learning how to produce small consumer items like shoes and umbrellas, which they sold on the side to help them subsidize their meager incomes. These items were made in small home or village operations even before Deng's reform policies came into play, and eager Wenzhou natives would travel to different parts of the country to sell their wares.

Not unlike the people of the Pearl River Delta region in Guangdong province, which encompasses such cities as Guangzhou, Shenzhen and Zhuhai, the natives of Wenzhou already had a culture of entrepreneurship. In 1984, when Deng opened the door for the city to become one of the coastal development areas, the Wenzhou people were quick to establish their own manufacturing and commercial centers. Today the city also produces electrical appliances and machinery; plastic, metal, chemical and leather products; and clothing and textiles. The Wenzhou businessmen have a reputation for being enterprising, to say the least, and are well known for their aggressive and cutthroat approach to business. They have also established a wide range of business interests overseas, including restaurants, retail shops and wholesale distributorships.

That innate acceptance of business travel made it natural and easy for the Christians to cross over or double as missionaries in their everyday lives, in effect becoming marketplace ministry practitioners. Wherever the believing Wenzhou businessmen traveled in China, they would discreetly seek out Christian communities and build bridges with other churches. If there were no fellowships in an area, they would start new gatherings and plant new churches with the people they met along the way.

The Church in Wenzhou is somewhat of an anomaly among the unregistered churches in China. This is due to the fact that the city and its surrounding area used to be more rural in its appearance and character. Hence the roots of this church technically lie in the rural house church itself. It may be hard for some to visualize this today given that there is so much wealth in the city and it boasts one of the highest per capita GDP rates in the nation. But before prosperity came to Wenzhou, the Christians here struggled to make ends meet just like their brothers and sisters elsewhere in the rural house church. Since the Open Door Policy was instituted, however, the city's GDP began to climb at an accelerated rate and, according to 2009 figures, had risen almost 200 times that in 1978.

The increasing wealth has had a direct impact on how the Church ministers in the city and beyond. While initially it was solely the traveling businessmen who planted house churches in the different areas they journeyed to, in response to the changing times, the Church today also sends out workers to preach the gospel and serve young people in university campuses throughout the country. One of the purposes, in so doing, is to provide support for the Christian Wenzhou students who leave home for higher education in other parts of China, to help minimize any feelings of detachment from family and friends they may experience, and to continue encouraging them in their personal walk with the Lord.

In turn, these students help to fulfill a second goal of the Wenzhou church in sending their workers out, which is to form part of the nucleus or base of a new church plant in the same city, be it Shanghai, Hangzhou or wherever. (Campus ministries, in fact, are widespread in China today; and whether the workers come from domestic fellowships or foreign organizations, they have made a significant contribution to the growth in the number of urban house churches.)

Further broadening the base of these college town church plants, according to Daniel, are the migrant workers who originate from the Wenzhou area. The ample supply of home believers transplanting themselves into the country's different cities, regardless of the reason—education or employment—has helped to facilitate the efforts of many Wenzhou church plants. A critical mass of members is swiftly achieved, and the church is allowed to take root in its new place. Overall, the greater prosperity has given the Church in Wenzhou a unique position as it comfortably straddles the rural customs and urban lifestyles.

The sheer concentration of believers who attend unregistered churches in the Wenzhou area has literally altered the landscape of the place. The underground fellowships here, for the most part, are above ground. They are not hidden; rather, their church buildings are very much visible, which again underlines the government's concern and desire to demolish religious buildings that belonged to unregistered assemblies at the turn of the millennium.

For all intents and purposes the early Wenzhou Church, or pre-Cultural Revolution Church, operated like and had the appearance of a rural underground fellowship. The people had a scant amount to live on, and the seeds for the dramatic growth to come, after 1976, were sown in the crucible of persecution. This is evidenced by the testimonies of the older generation of believers in the area—including the elder in Daniel's church—who were arrested, physically tortured and incarcerated for their faith during the years leading up to and including the Cultural Revolution.

Yet, the church came through the fire, and Daniel and his generation are the fruit of that faith and perseverance, emerging as the entrepreneurs, the factory owners, the networkers and the investors. They not only emerged, but they were also instrumental in helping the local Church bridge the old with the new, the archaic with the modern.

In Daniel's church, for example, the leadership has managed to successfully transition to the next generation, to move from purely rural house church practices to incorporate some urban ideas, and the church as a whole has adapted itself to remain relevant in their times. Today, they are a church network whose members number more than 10,000 believers around the country. Furthermore, Daniel and his generation of leaders tip the gender demographic in favor of the men—another aberration from the average underground church that is comprised mostly of female believers. In the last 30 years, even as the city of Wenzhou has been transformed and urbanized, so has its church.

基督教

"The anointing after suffering—that's the real anointing." Like Daniel, Abraham is not overly animated when he says this. Rather, he is a man who has learned a lesson, and he feels the reality of that epiphanic moment once again as he shares his experience.

Shortly after the Wanbang Church in Shanghai was shut down, the pastor decided that, with more time on his hands, he would take a trip and travel down to the city of Hangzhou. As he was driving along, he noticed that he had picked up a tail. At first he was surprised, and he repeatedly glanced into his rearview mirror to make sure he wasn't seeing things. He had heard about things like this happening to others, but he never expected that he would be an object of interest to anyone. He then decided to switch destinations in an effort to lose the tail. But upon rechecking his rearview mirror, he found he was still being followed. At that point, Abraham realized he had a very real and serious problem with the government. It was a grave situation, and he would need a miracle to get out of it. To that end, he came to the conclusion that he would need to fast and pray.

Wanbang Church was officially banned on November 10, 2009. The Minhang District in Shanghai issued the notice that was fastened to the front door of the church premises as if it were a restaurant condemned to closure for health violations—except in this case there would be no possibility of reopening.

Abraham's subsequent fast lasted for 40 days, and this period of abstinence from food proved to be life changing for him. Previously, Abraham had been accustomed to a jam-packed schedule every day. The agenda had been filled with responsibilities not only for his own church but also for ministry engagements and invitations from other fellowships around the country, where he provided Bible teaching or leadership training. As he describes it, he was always so busy "flying here and there." Without ever having taken a break since the church began—which was about a decade ago—he had not anticipated that a prolonged period of quiet could be so fulfilling or that a time of fasting and praying could be so rich.

"It was only in that time that I realized the anointing after suffering is the *real* anointing," he said again. "And what is real anointing? I used to think it was about having special power to prophesy, to bring healing or to perform miracles. But it's not. It's your desire, the actual desire and hunger you have for God, that becomes the life-changing force in you when you are challenged by hard times. Anointing comes so that we can be God-shaped, so that we can be made more like Him." He paused momentarily, and said, "Of course, throughout these difficulties our church has received lots of prayers from all over the world, and that has helped. But what we've gone through, the suffering and trials, it has actually been a blessing for all of us."

基督教

The trials Daniel and his church have experienced over the years have motivated them to focus deeper on the area of prayer. In practical terms, this involves praying for the wider Church in

China, as opposed to just praying for their own local needs, and reaching out to build links with other fellowships in an effort to create a larger united spiritual front. The Wenzhou church aims to connect with both urban and rural house churches.

"If one person can chase a thousand, or two people can put ten thousand to flight," says Daniel, quoting Deuteronomy 32:30, "the prayer of the Church as a whole should be even more powerful. The more believers that come together in unity, the stronger and bigger the collective faith, the more God will be able to do. So we are trying to encourage more churches to come together to pray."

In recent years, Daniel and his church have been at the forefront of unifying the largest house church movements in the country to pray together. While the networking with urban churches may not be a surprise, given the numerous traveling business-people and marketplace ministers coming from the area, and the general urbanization in progress around the country, they have been especially successful in establishing good relations with the rural house churches, including the largest streams, which are estimated to have millions of Christians.

Their own rural origins are no doubt a helpful factor here. In this time, they have organized and held prayer conferences in various cities and have had a 24-hour prayer chain in operation in Wenzhou since 2002. Though the house churches are scattered literally all over the country, Daniel believes the push for a unified prayer movement can give the whole Body of Christ a commonality, something they can all rally around and participate in as one. He recognizes that it's not something that can be achieved overnight, but it is vital to keep working at it. He cites Ezekiel 37 as a lesson for the Church in China. "The prophet sees a valley of dry bones," he explains, "but it's God who joins them together, gives them flesh, breathes life into them and makes them a viable force. In the long term, the unified prayer movement will gather momentum, and God will cause it to gain strength and bring blessing to China."

Prayer is considered one of the five main pillars of the rural house church in China, and Daniel fears that it is under threat of being lost in the younger and usually less mature urban assemblies. (The other four pillars are Bible-based teaching, evangelism, signs and wonders, and the willingness of believers to pay a price.) Prayer is the key, he says, because without it, there would be no anointing on the preaching of the Word, and no signs and wonders. While his church has evolved over the years—transforming its appearance and updating some of its methods to be relevant and to operate as an urban church—Daniel has not forgotten where their roots lie or what pillars hold it up. Throughout his church network, signs and wonders have been a regular occurrence, and he happily has plenty of stories to share.

The first story Daniel tells is of a young migrant girl who was sold by her uncle into prostitution at the age of 15. The girl wound up in the southern city of Shenzhen, in Guangdong province, where she also became a heroin addict and, over time, underwent more than one abortion. After a while, she was arrested by the police and sent back to her home village. While she was back in the village, someone shared the gospel with her and she became a believer, dedicating her heart to Jesus.

When she was 18 years old she decided to move, this time of her own volition, in an effort to find employment. She chose to go to Shanghai. But the conditions there were tough, and she fell into a depression. She could no longer see the purpose for her life, and in her despair she made several attempts to commit suicide, including cutting her wrists with a razor and climbing to the tops of tall buildings with the intention of jumping off the roof. In each of the latter attempts the only thing that stopped her from jumping was her fear of going to hell.

In time, the migrant girl received and accepted an invitation to come to a church that happened to be a part of Daniel's house church network. The believers prayed for her to be delivered from heroin addiction and the indescribable compulsion she had to commit suicide. It was a powerfully anointed time of prayer. Not only was she completely healed and delivered from dependence on drugs, but also all the scars from the razor cutting on her wrists spectacularly vanished right before everybody's eyes!

A few weeks later, the girl, now completely transformed, informed her new church that a Christian man had proposed marriage to her. In her heart she wanted to accept this man but feared to, because after her last abortion, she was informed that she would never be able to have a baby. She would not want to deprive her husband of a child. Daniel's co-workers then said they would pray for God to heal her womb. Once again, God was faithful and answered their prayers—for, sure enough, she was healed! Today the young woman is the mother of a healthy baby boy.

In another story Daniel told, a young man was dramatically delivered from demon possession and saved. The man, in his mid-20s, lived with his father in a hut on the outskirts of a village near Wenzhou. Situated beside a wooded area, it was a dirty, rancid place that the rest of the villagers tended to shun. But one day, a disciple of Daniel's visited the village and learned of the existence of this father and son. He asked to be taken to their place so that he could share the gospel with them. Upon seeing people approach their home, the father and son got up and ran away into the woods. When Daniel's disciple and his team found no one at home, they decided to kneel down outside the little home and pray.

After some time, the younger man came back out of curiosity. Approaching his home with some timidity, he looked like a wild jungle man. He was filthy and smelly, clearly having not showered or bathed in a long time. His hair was greasy and had grown down to his waist, and it was a tangled mess. For clothes, he wore tattered rags. Daniel's disciple was not put off for a second, though. With an inviting smile on his face, he walked up to the young man, amiably greeted him by putting his arm around his shoulders and warmly embraced him. The whole team gathered loosely around and began to pray for the young man and praise God for him.

As the minutes passed, the young man grew increasingly uncomfortable, visibly squirming and agitated. He then began shaking uncontrollably, struggling and flailing his arms. Undeterred, the Christians persisted in their praying until at last the young man became calm and still, and then he broke down and wept. While his tears were drying, Daniel's disciple gently began to explain the gospel to him, and then he led him to the Lord. Today the prayers continue for the father—that he, too, would come to the knowledge of God's saving grace and that the son would be able to grow and mature in his faith.

In yet another example of the signs and wonders that happen throughout his church network, Daniel shared the testimony of a co-worker and his family that lived and served the church in the city of Ningpo. After establishing several house churches there, he had been arrested and sentenced to five years in prison because of his faith. While he was serving this term, his wife and five-year-old daughter underwent their own share of struggles. Every day they were ostracized by their community, treated as outcasts, because it was known that a member of their family had been charged, found guilty and incarcerated. Even his daughter was excluded by her kindergarten classmates.

His wife fell ill during this period and was diagnosed with systemic lupus erythematosus. The illness meant that she had to stay out of the sun because it grievously aggravated the lesions and other skin disorders she had developed from the disease. For most of the time, she was unable to step foot out of doors; otherwise, her skin would literally peel off her face, and she could only find comfort by staying at home with the air conditioning on. She was utterly demoralized and felt as if she were "as ugly as the Phantom of the Opera." But the believers from her church began to pray for her healing. Prayer teams from the house church network joined in as well, including Daniel, and over time, she began to heal. The skin disorders cleared up, her skin was made beautifully smooth once again, and today the disease is completely gone from her body.

In a final example, Daniel recalls one of the three-day fasting and prayer sessions in his own church. A brother by the name of Hung attended and requested prayer for healing. A thin and ill-looking man, Hung stood before the people gathered there and told them that he had recently been to hospitals for medical tests and consultations in both Wenzhou and Shanghai. In both cities the doctors confirmed his diagnosis of lung cancer. His disease was considered to be in the final stages, and there was nothing more they could do for him except to prescribe some medicine to help relieve a bit of the pain. The doctors recommended that he return home and prepare to die.

Of course the church agreed to pray and fast for Hung over the next three days. Hung also continued to attend the meetings, despite his condition. On the third day, when he arrived at the church, the people thought their brother was looking better than he had the previous two days; he was livelier and appeared less tired and haggard. He confirmed that he was "very much alive" indeed, and he shared with the church how he felt like a huge stone had been removed from him. Previously, he said, it was as if the stone had been tied to his body; it had weighed him down. But now, when he awoke that day, it was gone! It had been completely taken away! He said it used to feel like he was being held under bondage of some sort, but now he was relieved and totally set free from it.

Hung was sure this burden was related to the cancer in his body. If the burden was now gone, the cancer must be gone too. So, as soon as he could, he went back to see the doctors in Wenzhou and Shanghai. They checked and tested him again. They reviewed and rechecked the results. Finally, they concluded that the cancer cells in Hung's body had been greatly reduced and he seemed to be recovering very well. It was amazing!

Hung came back to the church and excitedly reported what had happened at the hospitals. He also said that he was no longer taking any medications, and he had returned to work and was feeling very, very good.

"Once we lose our fervency for all-night prayer meetings and fasting," Daniel reiterates, "we lose our power to go out and do exploits in His name."

Daniel also believes the timing for the unified prayer movement is crucial. "There has certainly been revival in the church," he says, "but the truth is that there has also been revival in traditional religions, like Daoism and Buddhism. Christians need to be aware of the reality of the spiritual realm. Our struggle is not against flesh and blood," he said, quoting from the book of Ephesians, chapter 6, "but against the powers of this dark world and against the spiritual forces of evil in the heavenly realms. We're soldiers in the Lord's army. We can't just always be praying to preserve ourselves."

基督教

Undoubtedly, the survival instinct of the house church in China is strong. Tested and proved, that instinct has been well honed through the hardships of the years prior to Deng Xiaoping's economic reforms, and perseverance has been upheld as a true value. This is the way Daniel was raised in the faith, since he converted to Christianity during the Cultural Revolution.

He was 12 years old when he accepted Christ. His mother was sick in the hospital with bronchitis, and a relative who was a believer came to visit her. After the relative shared the gospel and prayed with her, his mother became a Christian. She recovered from her illness soon afterward and entreated her whole family to believe in Jesus. They did.

Daniel was baptized in water a few years later and felt a prompting within him to serve the Lord. In response, the teenager began to preach at secret meetings. One of those meetings was on a hill, where he and his fellow believers were subsequently discovered and surrounded by several hundred Red Guards. As a result, he came under tremendous pressure at school. Daniel was stripped of his membership in the Youth Communist League, and teachers and students alike constantly tried to convince (and at times intimidate) him into not believing in Jesus anymore. One teacher was especially avid in his efforts. He promised Daniel that if he would give up his faith, he would ensure that Daniel was assigned a good job after graduation. He would even act as a matchmaker for Daniel and help him find a wife. Now those were tantalizing promises for a young teen from a poor family looking to embark on manhood. Career and economic prospects in Wenzhou were dismal in the 1970s; and marriage, in Chinese society, was one of the most important goals in life. Nevertheless, Daniel overcame the temptations and refused to renounce his faith.

基督教

"Nobody can keep their faith at a high level forever, not even a pastor," says Benjamin, Abraham's right-hand man. Benjamin is 30 years old, though he looks like a first-year university student. He is telling his version of the official eradication of Wanbang Church. An only son who worked for the family business in Hubei province, he was in Shanghai on a business trip one day in 2004 when his client invited him to a church. Always aiming to please his client, young Benjamin acquiesced. He was subsequently introduced to Jesus Christ and saved.

Eventually, Benjamin left the family business to serve the Lord full time and has been working with Abraham and the Wanbang Church for several years now. He has been instrumental in coordinating the training of the cell groups, which helped to spark the church's explosive growth from about 300 members to 1,500 in just three years. He has also helped to train other cell group leaders in roughly a dozen other churches in various cities, including Hangzhou, Wenzhou, Hefei, Luoyang and Guilin.

"As a church leader," says Benjamin, "you're aware that there may be pressure from the government at times. Lay members don't usually think about this. I think it's naturally more on your mind when you work for the church."

Benjamin pauses to find the right words. It is an effort to control his emotions as the injuries resurface in recalling the memories. It was the first time in his life that his faith had been tested in this way, and the whole experience is still a bit too close for comfort. But he manages to steel himself, and continues, "At first you think everything will be okay when the pressure comes, because you have strong relationships with the people, especially with your cell group members. You believe they are your friends. On the other hand, you also think it's exciting. It's like James Bond—every guy likes to dream he's a hero like James Bond—you have to find a way to outsmart the police and not get caught. After all, how would you know if you're a real Christian without persecution? So you think, *Come on, bring it on! I have faith! I can handle this!*"

Benjamin went on to describe the raid on the church by the police. The church was located in a commercial building. It happened at midnight. He and a handful of others were still working in the office. There were also a number of elderly women in another room who always kept a prayer vigil going for the church. In total, about 20 Wanbang members were on the church premises. When the police came, they outnumbered the church members by roughly three to one. They destroyed the security cameras and seized all the computers and other files.

In the days that followed, Benjamin, as part of the church's leadership team, found himself under tight official surveillance. To begin with, he discovered problems with his email: New messages had already been read before he'd seen them, and a lot of people were experiencing bounce-backs when they sent their messages to him. His phone calls were also monitored, as he discerned during the course of his police interviews, which occurred on a monthly basis for half a year.

The interviews were conducted by several police precincts and varying levels of authority—city, provincial and federal. Was there a difference among them? Generally speaking, if the interviewers were from the higher levels, they would tend to be more polite, asking Benjamin, for example, when they could have tea together. If the questioning was from officials of lower or municipal authority, Benjamin usually found himself yelled at and rudely treated.

"After the first month, the passion is still strong," says Benjamin. "You still feel like nothing can bring your faith down. After a few months, though, you start to feel very tired. The tiredness is spiritual, mental and physical, because you feel you can never let your guard down when you're under surveillance, not even once."

Another complication to his trials was the fact that Benjamin's parents are not Christians. As the only son, Chinese tradition dictates that he must excel in his career and prosper in life for the sake of family honor. When Benjamin decided to resign from the family business to work for a church, his parents viewed the new job as an unprofitable vocation. It was a hard pill for them to swallow. Needless to say, this decision put an added strain on the filial relationship.

A further blow was the fact that he had decided not to live at home anymore, but wanted to relocate to another city. In their eyes it was an unnecessary move, because the family was fine financially—it was not as if they were a poor farming family trying to make ends meet out in the sticks.

When his parents visited or phoned him, it was hard for Benjamin to live with the obvious disappointment he saw in their faces and heard in their voices. His parents could not understand why he chose to work at something that would not make him money and thus affect his marriage prospects. There was one occasion that especially stuck with Benjamin: That was when his mother visited him in Shanghai and couldn't stop crying when she saw the apartment her son was living in. It was nowhere near as nice as at home.

Benjamin loves his parents and doesn't want to displease them, but he also knows that he is called to serve the Lord. Yet, with the banning of the church and the official scrutiny he and the other leaders have come under, there has been no way for him to tell his parents that he has been experiencing pressure from the government. It has been a hard and very lonely journey.

Every cloud has a silver lining. Benjamin has taken a difficult situation and found some good. Because he has been seeing so many policemen, he figures that God is using him to connect with them. "They don't know who Jesus is," he says as if he can't understand how such a situation like this could possibly exist. He holds out both of his hands, half in wonder and half in a shrug. "They don't know what a Christian is." So Benjamin has been taking these new opportunities to share his testimony with them and to tell them about the gospel. "Some of them," he says, "not everyone, but some of them, are my friends now."

He has also received a deeper understanding of grace and what it means to forgive. "I've learned how to bless three kinds of people," Benjamin says. "First are the people who persecute me. With all my heart I can bless them." He says this ardently. "Second, I can bless those who have abandoned the church. They left when the church needed them most, but I forgive them. The third group is those who betrayed the church. They were the hardest for me to forgive. But I bless them now."

Benjamin says that those long six months of surveillance were like going to a big conference.

A conference?

"Yeah," he recalls, "it was a time for learning. I learned how to bless and forgive from my heart those who persecuted me and those who betrayed me. It was not easy. It was really hard." He begins to speak with growing assertiveness. "There was an unbelievable amount of pressure, but that is where the anointing came from, through the pressure times. Nobody can take that anointing away. Nobody."

基督教

When Daniel was Benjamin's age, he faced another kind of pressure. The nation's family planning policy was threatening the life of his unborn child. His wife was about halfway through her pregnancy, and the couple was desperate to find a way to ensure their baby's survival before people could see she was expecting.

The notorious one-child policy, introduced in 1978, did not apply to the entire population, contrary to popular perception in the West. There were some exceptions, such as for ethnic minorities and rural couples. Because Daniel and his wife's *hukou* or residency permits were from the countryside, they were actually allowed to have two children. But they were not allowed to have a third. If the authorities discovered that his wife was pregnant this time, she would be forced to have an abortion.

In a situation somewhat reminiscent of the Bible's account of baby Moses surviving the pharaoh's edict of death in ancient Egypt, the couple prayed earnestly for wisdom about their situation and eventually came up with a plan. Daniel would search for a remote village where his wife could hide away until their child was born. Then mother and baby would return home. The officials would not kill a baby once he or she had been born; they would only fine the parents, which Daniel and his wife were more than willing to pay.

Through his connections with some rural churches in neighboring Anhui province, where he sometimes went to teach at churches, the husband found a place of refuge for his wife and child. The only thing left was to transport them there.

Despite the boom in construction and development in the southeast part of China, in the 1980s, there were still many areas that had yet to begin their urbanization, and many roads were waiting to be built. Consequently, there were no paved roads to the village they were headed for in Anhui. After a 19-hour train ride in the hard seats, followed by another four hours on a cramped, overcrowded bus to the nearest county town, Daniel had to ride a bike, doubling with his wife, on a long, uneven and muddy road, for most of the following day. It was slow going as the bike was difficult to maneuver over the bumpy country lane, and Daniel's wife experienced much pain and discomfort throughout the journey. But they made it to their destination.

Several months later, the baby was born; and the rest, as they say, is history. "Praise God," the husband and wife both say, "the baby was safe! Today he is a healthy, full-grown adult, and he's serving the Lord. This is really God's grace."

Many of the Christians in Wenzhou are firm believers in God's ability to perform miracles in individual circumstances like this, to divinely intervene and make a way in a calamitous situation. In fact, many people in this city have come to know Christ because of the signs and wonders they've witnessed or experienced firsthand. It is because of such demonstrations of the Holy Spirit's power that faith has been able to arise and has birthed so many rural house churches throughout the last 60-odd years of the Chinese Church. Wenzhou's church, of course, has its roots in the rural fellowship, and Daniel does not hesitate to pay tribute to the many faithful who have stepped up to serve those individuals in need.

"Many of our brothers and sisters have humbly served one on one," he says. "They hear of a sick person and quietly go to their home or wherever they are to help the person and pray for him or her. Then the person gets healed and his home becomes a new place of fellowship. That's generally how a new church gets planted." There was a wide grin on Daniel's face as he made this last statement.

基督教

In the last 30 years, the principles guiding Daniel's ministry have not changed. At times they may be packaged differently, but the core remains the same. As a young man, he began his full-time service to the Lord as—how he describes it—a "beggar evangelist." He literally had no income or regular means of support, yet this was no deterrent to do what he knew he was called to do, namely preach the good news and build the Lord's Church. So he did just that, faithfully and wholeheartedly, the best that he knew how and without thought for himself. Obeying the Lord's calling was all that mattered to him.

In due course, an elder in the church arranged Daniel's marriage to a young woman who happened to be gifted with business savvy. His new wife became his support base: She established a factory with her family that manufactured electronic switches, plugs and cables. As a result, the young preacher was free to continue his ministry without any worries or care given to where or when his next bowl of rice would come.

At the same time, as the years went by, Daniel was able to develop his own business instincts. Today his preaching ministry regularly takes him around the country, and he continues to help maintain the family enterprise. He has other business interests, too, including some overseas. These usually double as a means to facilitate ministry in these foreign lands, to forge new beachheads for the Church, including, like Ruth, in the mission field. The Church in Wenzhou, though, has had a bit of a head start because they've been sending out businesspeople since the 1980s. Until recently, the vast majority of them journeyed solely within Chinese borders. Increasingly now, the Church is looking beyond to cross-cultural mission fields.

"It won't be easy," Daniel says of the missions task ahead. "But that's one reason why we face suffering—it helps to make us stronger, and God gives us grace to deal with it. When we are weak, He is strong, as Paul the apostle says. So we will not lose heart. Though outwardly we are wasting away, yet inwardly we are being renewed day by day."

Abraham agrees. "Suffering in the church is a blessing," the pastor from Shanghai says. "But it's a hard truth to accept. The natural tendency is to walk away when we have to suffer, to try to avoid it. But if the church doesn't suffer, it won't grow. I was meditating, and this thought came to me," he continued. "If our church can't handle what we're going through now, how will we cope when we get to the mission field?"

"It's normal for a Christian to suffer," says Daniel. "Jesus suffered. The more suffering we face, the more we can feel that God is giving us extra strength to deal with it. We can really feel the

Lord's presence in those times. He is with us." Daniel's words are an echo of what Abraham and Benjamin have been saying about anointing. "Even though the Church faces persecution in China, we can see that God has appointed this," he continues. "So we won't have hatred toward the people who persecute us, and we'll pray for them and for the government. We bless them. That's what the Word of God teaches us."

"Persecution is a must for the churches in China," Abraham interjects here. "It's a required class or lesson that Christians have to go through. If believers can understand the value of persecution, that it brings blessings to the Church and can help them grow individually, then we will be so much stronger in faith and unity. Ultimately, persecution brings health and growth to the Church, and more glory to the Lord."

"I will serve Him through all my life," Daniel says in conclusion. "Me and my household, we will serve the Lord."

Note
1. Source: Asia Harvest.

Christian

CH基督教NA

AND THE LIGHT OF THE WORLD

The Great Sichuan Earthquake struck on May 12, 2008. With a magnitude of 7.9 the destruction was widespread, including churches. As of July 2008, the natural disaster left 69,197 dead, 374,176 injured and more than 18,000 missing.

The Great Sichuan Earthquake (continued).

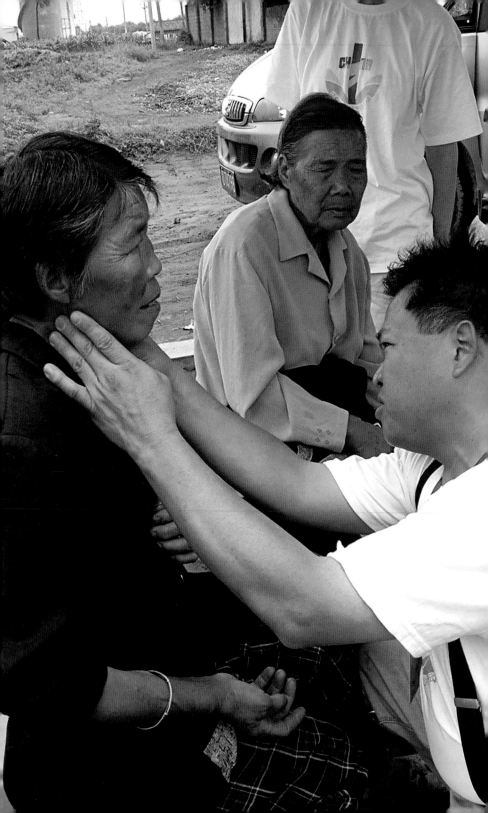

More than 3,000 Christians came from around the country to help the victims in Sichuan in a unified effort under the China ActionLove Volunteers Association banner (flag in the center). The Christian effort impressed the government and was later acknowledged by President Hu Jintao at a special banquet in Beijing.

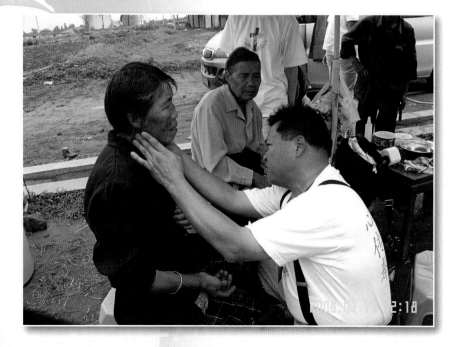

Caleb and his church were among those who helped under the China ActionLove Volunteers Association banner.

Paul and his team pray before they begin another day of relief work.

Job and his team were among those who remained after the aid and relief teams left; they helped the community rebuild. Daniel's church presents then-Director General of Social Welfare and Charity Promotion for China's Ministry of Civil Affairs, Dr. Wang Zhenyao (wearing the suit), with a donation for the earthquake victims.

In Wenzhou the large number of unregistered churches, whose buildings are now visible, has literally altered the landscape of the place. In Daniel's church, for instance, there is room to accommodate more than 3,500 worshipers.

In Shanghai, after Wanbang Church was officially banned at the end of 2008, the members of the church gathered outside for their meetings for a while.

Abraham lays hands on and prays for people.

BELOW: In Xiamen, the son of Mr. and Mrs. Cai was involved in a motor vehicle accident which left him in a coma for 2 months. He awoke in a persistent vegetative state and remained that way for more than half of a year. Paul's church began to pray for his healing and, miraculously, today he is walking with a frame. His awe-inspiring healing led to 10 different families coming to know Jesus Christ. ABOVE: Ruth baptizes a new believer in Wuhan.

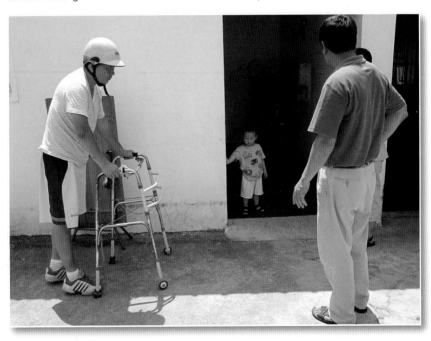

6

The Model
Worshiper

Isaac turned to Abraham and said, "Father?"
"Yes, my son?" Abraham replied.
"We have the fire and the wood," the boy said,
"but where is the sheep for the burnt offering?"
"God will provide a sheep for the burnt offering, my son,"
Abraham answered. And they both walked on together.

GENESIS 22:7-8

"WHAT YOU SEE IN CHINA is similar to the situation in South Korea," Abraham says. He is talking about the state of the Church in the two Asian nations, referring to the fact that there have traditionally been two streams feeding Protestant Christianity in both the People's Republic and the Land of the Morning Calm. In one stream, the practices and traditions of the faithful have been well ordered, with a clear structure and, to some, a leaning to the conservative, or orthodox, side. This is the legacy of the overseas missionaries, he says, the Anglicans, the Baptists, and so forth. In terms of China, this would typically be seen in the formality and more ritualistic practices of the Three Self Patriotic Movement church.

In the second stream, there has been less ceremony. If one were to go from assembly to assembly, one would find no consistently employed model of worship: The type of meeting place can vary; the preaching can appear haphazard and be different in style of delivery, presentation and breadth of understanding.

Sometimes there is not even a pastor. Yet, undeniably, there is liveliness and dynamism in the fellowships, which are often characterized by miracles, healings and visions. This is usually what one would find in the rural house church in the PRC.

"But," says Abraham, "the route we are taking in the city is a new way. It takes a little bit from the traditional. It takes a bit from the evangelical and charismatic. And all around China today, you can see that churches from every stream are becoming more open to making changes. Even some of the Three Self churches are becoming more broad-minded and less rigid, and some of the rural churches are trying to move toward a more solid structure. University fellowships also have their own ideas for worship models, as do the people in the marketplace."

In essence, Abraham was saying, the twenty-first century churches in the PRC, regardless of stream and whether or not they are registered, have developed the habit of learning from each other—borrowing ideas from each other and from overseas in an effort to be more contemporary and to fit in with the changing society around them.

Abraham's cognizance of the different ways of "doing church" began in the days when he was a student at a TSPM seminary. While studying there, he decided to research the actual models of worship that existed in the nation. In visiting hundreds of churches in the process, Abraham came to the conclusion that, in general, the TSPM model was lacking in substance (it has too much of what he calls an "A-B-C emphasis"—Attendance, Buildings, Cash) and that the rural underground fellowships did not address all the urban needs. So when the time came for Abraham to begin his church in Shanghai, at the turn of the millennium, he chose to break with both those conventions. "As a result," he says with a laugh, "we made many wrong turns." Eventually, the church found a feasible path to follow for growth in the emphasis of discipleship.

Midway through the first decade of the 2000s, Abraham and the leadership team began to emphasize training their laypeople to motivate them to get involved in the ministry of their church and to take ownership of it. (Traditionally, the TSPM relies on formal clergy alone to serve in their assemblies, while the house church tends to be more disorganized in their methods and inconsistent in their implementation.) This led to a new problem: no outlets for the trained people to serve. That was when Abraham learned the value of the cell group. Their disciples were then released into service in the cell groups with two leaders appointed per group.

After a while, he began to further espouse the value of "one body with many parts" by facilitating the development of strategic prayer teams to minister to the individual needs of the congregants, which further supported the growth of the church. The result, he says, is that the burden of prayer no longer lay solely with the senior leadership of the church, but was shouldered by a wider group of believers. (Initially, when the church began its explosive growth, he and his fellow pastors were responsible for praying for all the individual needs in the church.) It has also meant that people who are gifted in the area of prayer are better utilized, which is a further blessing to the church. As an example, he told a story about a young woman in their congregation.

This young lady was 21 years old and had been born deaf, but she had learned how to read lips. At church she would always sit opposite the speaker so that she could see what he was saying and understand what was going on throughout the service. One day, while visiting her cell group, the lady asked Abraham to pray for her to receive the ability to hear. So, of course, he did.

Over the next several weeks, one of the strategic prayer teams from the church continued to pray for and with her. These prayer teams are strategic in the sense that they consist of a combination of people who each exercise different spiritual gifts. One person, for instance, might operate in the gift of knowledge; another might regularly use the gift of healing; and still another, the gift of faith. Regardless of which team, however, each member operates in a different area of strength. No one member carries the responsibility of ministry alone; they work together, sharing the burden of caring for the needy person, and each one has a unique role to play.

One day, on her way back from church with her mother, the young woman suddenly uttered a word. It wasn't enunciated very clearly, but even so, words began to come out of her mouth. "Mama," she said with growing excitement, "I hear you. I can hear!" Her hearing was completely restored! It was an absolute joy and wonder to both the mother and daughter, and today the young woman is an active member of the praise and worship team at church.

Within three years, starting from 2006, the church grew rapidly with this cell group and team model, more than doubling each year to reach 1,500 members by 2009. Abraham believes that had the church not been officially banned, they would have grown to 3,000 congregants in the next year. "However," he says laughingly again, "it's still good. We would have had a problem if we grew to several thousand. God wants to see fruit; but even more important, He wants to have my heart. He wants me. No matter how much fruit I bear, if my heart is not all and totally God's, He won't get all the glory. I'll end up stealing His glory—and that is not right."

基督教

Abraham is a fourth generation Christian in his family, born of Chaoxian or Korean descent, one of the official minority groups in China. The Chaoxian people mainly live in the northeast of the country, in Heilongjiang, Jilin and Liaoning provinces, though they can also be found in other parts of the country, including Inner Mongolia.

In Abraham's family tree, the first to be saved was his great-grandfather, who became a church elder. His mother, too, was a church leader. While growing up, Abraham regularly accompanied his mother to church meetings and witnessed miraculous healings and deliverances from demon possession. Despite the lineage of faith, though, it wasn't until 1989 that Abraham began to take his relationship with Christ seriously. Up to that point, God was a faraway concept to the young man—God was real but distant, and not concerned with him personally. Yet, the events of Tiananmen Square triggered a deep soul-searching journey for the fresh university graduate of business management.

Four years later, the search culminated at a hospital, where Abraham spent two months recovering from a motorbike accident in which he broke his leg. The doctor had chosen not to set his leg in a cast, so the young man was confined to lying in a bed for days on end. In severe pain, the only thing he could do with some degree of comfort was listen to the Walkman his mother had brought him. The cassettes she supplied him were all of Christian praise and worship music, and Abraham began to contemplate the meaning of his life. What was he doing? Where was he heading?

At the time of the accident, Abraham was employed at a bank during the day and, like other creatively enterprising Chinese of his generation, engaged in a side business after hours. He happened to be helping friends with logistics in their car smuggling business, which was stocked by vehicles stolen from Japan and then conveyed via the PRC for redistribution and sale in North Korea. That was, in fact, how he had broken his leg. He had been in the process of "transporting the goods" when he crashed.

Upon release from the hospital, and after many prayers from his mother and her fellow church members, Abraham committed his life to Christ and promptly enrolled at a TSPM seminary for Bible training. After only two months of study, he was expelled after he became involved in a physical altercation and beat up a fellow student. Back in the dorm that same day, to pack up his belongings, he fell victim to a freak accident in which the cap of a marker pen flicked toward his face, shattered his eyeglasses and cut his cornea.

Abraham found himself in another hospital, where another doctor informed him that surgery would be the only way to repair his bleeding eye. But there was no guarantee, he was informed, that the surgery would completely fix the injury. It was a sobering moment, and Abraham began to consider the possibility of life without sight in one of his eyes. At that particular moment, he says, he was primarily concerned for his mom. What would she think? He was worried about her because his younger sister had already lost the sight in one of her eyes in an accident when she was seven years old. The memory of how much his mother had cried weighed heavily on his mind.

He and some students began to pray fervently, and Abraham repented of his fighting and bad attitude at school up to that point. He vowed to God that no matter what happened to his eye, even if he were to lose his sight, he would still serve God and preach the gospel. After the prayers, he felt a tremendously deep sense of peace.

The next day, Abraham awoke to find that his eye had miraculously healed overnight! The bleeding had stopped and his sight had been restored without surgery, as verified by the doctor back at the hospital, and he knew that God had confirmed his calling. So he went back to the school, knocked on the dean's door and told him what God had done. He couldn't go home now, he pleaded; he had a calling to obey and wanted to keep attending the course of study. Moved by the exuberant passion and clear change of heart in this young man, the dean reinstated Abraham, who went on to complete the course.

Abraham was now so motivated to serve God that in between school terms he would go to preach in the countryside. It is not unusual to find churches in rural areas that do not have full-time ministers; so when the young, eager Bible student showed up, they gladly allowed him to speak. They welcomed anyone who could teach them more about the Bible. Abraham would often be invited back the following week, which at first caused him to worry, as he wasn't sure what topic or portion of Scripture he could possibly speak on next. But somehow he found something to teach, and God was faithful.

In some places, there would be less than two dozen believers in the church when he arrived. Yet Abraham was not discouraged, and he preached with all his heart to the few in attendance. A few spontaneous decisions were made in some places to hold additional meetings afterward, as the little churches found that they really liked what they were hearing from the young man. It soon became a normal occurrence that two or three extra meetings would be tagged on, with the services running over consecutive days, and the church members would invite their friends and relatives from the surrounding areas. In these instances it became fairly customary for Abraham to see the congregation more than triple in size by the end of the last meeting.

One day, he arrived at his grandmother's village in the Yanbian Korean Autonomous Prefecture in Jilin province. Here he met a group of people at random on the street and began to share the gospel with them. As was the new normal pattern, this first gathering turned into several more, and then the group decided to invite him to be their pastor. Abraham accepted, and this became the first church he ever planted. Because he was still a student, when the new semester began, he commuted every Sunday between the seminary and his grandma's village to minister to the church. The commute involved a one-and-a-half-hour train ride plus 30 minutes on a bus each way. "It was amazing," Abraham says with a laugh. "I didn't know anything about the Bible, and I was preaching."

基督教

The 40-day fast that came about as a result of the Wanbang Church shutdown was a time of extensive reflection for Abraham. It was a time of taking stock and of examining the heart. Ultimately, Abraham came to alter his views in a number of key areas. His understanding of church growth and development, and Christian leadership specifically, underwent closer scrutiny. Take, for starters, the structure and management of the church.

"Before the shutdown," says Abraham, using the metaphor of a supermarket, "Wanbang was structured like a Walmart. (Walmart has everything, and shoppers don't need to go anywhere else to find what they're looking for—there's clothes, food, entertainment, medicine, furniture—you name it.) Lots of people came to Wanbang, this one big, fully stocked central meeting place. We had our own teaching, of course, but also Christian books, music and other resources from around the world to help a person grow in his or her faith. But the vast majority of churches in China are more like family-run stores, and they have a much smaller selection of goods. In these small shops there is a lot of human contact; everyone knows each other. And if you don't have enough money to pay one day, the storekeeper will still let you take the product home and bring the money in the next day. They're relaxed about it."

He continues with the metaphor. "In family-run shops, the management style will vary from store to store, and inventory policies and administration practices will differ. But in a supermarket, it's very organized about how things are done. From a customer's point of view, it's tougher if you need help from them, if you are looking for the personal connection. If you don't have the money, for instance, they won't let you take the goods with you. They are more rigid in their policies and less flexible in their practices. Prices may be cheaper at the 'Walmart,' and the selection of goods wider, but human relationships tend to be more impersonal, more distant, and a lot of management efforts are directed toward devising systems to keep things moving."

So how exactly have his views on structure and management changed?

"Now," says Abraham, "I lean toward a convenience store chain model for the church, more akin to 7-Eleven." A convenience store takes the best of the supermarket and family models, he explains. It takes the organization and consistent management approach of the large supermarket and mixes the friendlier and closer human relationship aspects of the small shops. With the convenience store model, there would be a gathering in different suburbs or neighborhoods, but they would have the same compatible management style and consistent policies and products to offer.

The ethos or values of the church have also come under review as a result of the shutdown and Abraham's reflections from his fast. Before the time of testing, the church had been in the habit of purchasing and translating books for their discipleship teaching from leading overseas Christian pastors, including from the West. What Abraham found after a closer inspection was that the emphasis of some of this teaching was not ideal for his church's situation. To begin with, the cultural context of the teaching was unlike that of China's. The behaviors and reactions to situations by Chinese people have been shaped and molded by completely different traditions and historical circumstances, creating a frame of reference that is incompatible with those teachings.

Upon deeper meditation of the materials, Abraham felt that there were other, more important emphases—for example, the understanding of a leader's authority. He has concluded that "the authority that arises from the impact of Christ in one's life is much more powerful and meaningful than the authority that is bestowed with a title or position."

Another emphasis is the understanding of fear. "Fear is not about number two being afraid of number one, and number three worrying about how number two will react. To truly fear God is to revere Him, to give Him respect. When we fear God, we need to recognize and acknowledge that He is greater than we are. It is humbling when we realize who He really is in relationship to us. Even Confucius said there are three fears," he says with growing earnestness, "fear of heaven, fear of authority and fear of the word of a saint—that is, an elder's wisdom or teaching. And we are now learning what it really means to fear God. He is the King of kings, and He is certainly higher and wiser than all of us."

Abraham has also come to realize that bigger and more do not necessarily mean better. In the aftermath of the shutdown, the size of the Wanbang congregation dropped from 1,500 to about 500. This, not surprisingly, had a direct impact on the church's bottom line. Instead of the reduced finances becoming a worry, however, Abraham was surprised at what he discovered.

When there were 1,500 people, the church collection amounted to roughly a couple hundred thousand *renminbi* per month. Annually, that came to a total somewhere in the neighborhood of a few million *renminbi*. From month to month the tithes and offerings would be just enough to cover the expenses of running the church, including the cost of the building, equipment, special materials, translations, printing and administration. As the pastor, he was used to seeing very little, if anything, left over after all the bills were paid each month.

With the diminished congregation, their collections brought in considerably less than they were used to seeing. However, Abraham has found that the church actually has more money left over at the end of the month. This is due to the fact that since the church structure has gone "7-Eleven," except for the odd special occasion, they no longer have to pay for the building, maintenance and all the equipment and special materials it took to keep the large-scale meetings and operations running. Moreover, those leftover funds are sufficient for the church to send and support co-workers in the mission field. Indeed, on the last day of his 40-day fast, the church actually sent its first missionary abroad—to Thailand. In the course of the year that followed, they commissioned and sent out several more.

"Our church is All Nations." When Abraham says this he is referring to the fact that the translation of the Chinese (pinyin) word "Wanbang" means "all nations." He continues, "This name was chosen for the church because our goal was to minister to the nations. We've been a church for more than 10 years, but we only sent our first [full-time] missionary out in 2010." (He doesn't count the short-term trips.) "If we hadn't gone through the persecution, we would have kept going on in the same way, the same direction, the same methods; and we probably wouldn't have sent out any missionaries at all. Sometimes I feel ashamed when I think of this. But that's another reason God allows suffering, to help us learn lessons."

Wanbang used to spend the money to grow the *operations* of the church; today they are actually able to provide real support and make a genuine investment into their people, whether those people are members or co-workers. "That seems to be a better way to use the money," says Abraham. "Wouldn't you agree?"

Worship is yet another area that came under review during his time of reflection. Abraham says, "I was watching Good TV, a Christian television station broadcast out of Taiwan. I was watching Joel Osteen and other churches from the United States, Taiwan and South Korea. You can see they're really into their praise and worship music. It's very touching to watch them worship this way. And when I visit overseas churches, I can see that the facilities are good in their buildings—they have lots of musical instruments and sound equipment. We used to try to have all that in our church too. So after we were banned, when I saw all this on TV, or when I visited churches abroad, I couldn't help but wonder if the people in those places would still be able to praise and worship God in the same way if they were under pressure from the authorities, if they were under persecution. Then this made me wonder, *What is true worship?* Because, when the church was shut down, we didn't have a building anymore. We don't have instruments and lots of musicians. We don't have a sound system. I wondered, *Does this mean we aren't worshiping God or that our worship is of less value to Him?*

"But then I came to see that true worship happens all the time," he says. "It happens when I'm with my family, when I'm eating food or reading the Bible. It can even happen when I'm sleeping. True worship is how I live my life before God. When I'm living it in spirit and in truth—that is true worship. That is the worship the Father seeks."

Abraham says that this whole experience has been a time of learning humility and what it truly means to let Jesus shine through him. Before the ban, he had great confidence and faith in his own abilities as a pastor. Today, he says, he is learning how to rely on God more.

"I used to think that the growth we saw in our church was because of this wonderful model I had designed. I visited South Korea before and thought that if Yonggi Cho can build a big church, I can too." He smiles as he remembers this. "I tried to copy some of his methods here in China, and they worked for a little while. But then I must have hit a raw nerve somewhere in the Chinese government, because then all the pressure came on us. With the banning of the church, I've basically been snubbed out, erased. I'm not the pastor of the largest urban church anymore. I'm not successful anymore.

"Did God allow this persecution to happen for the sake of the church or for myself?" Abraham asks philosophically. "I had the largest unregistered church," he answers. "I was considered a successful pastor. If it were up to me, I would have kept that position for a long time. But then God used the Communist government to humble me, and now I am a servant wanting to learn more from Him.

"This whole experience," Abraham concludes, "has been a kind of distillation, a cleansing. We had to get rid of all the unnecessary, unpleasing things before God. What I've learned is that I shouldn't be copying Korean pastors, Western pastors or anyone else. What they do is in, and for, a totally different cultural context." He pauses momentarily. "The most important thing for me now is to follow *God's* vision of growth for the Church in China. He has a specific plan and context for us. We need to continue purifying ourselves and continue the path of the previous generations that experienced explosive growth in the past 60 years. And if that means suffering, then we will learn those lessons too."

Abraham went on to describe other changes in his life, such as being able to spend more time with his wife and children. Previously, it had been a struggle for him to squeeze in dinner with the whole family even a couple of times a week, and there hadn't been much interaction between father and children. The bulk of parenting, up to that point, had been left in his wife's hands. The church's shutdown, however, has led to an enriching time for them all, and they've drawn closer together as a family unit. Father and children better understand and support each other now.

His vision has been expanded. He sees himself with more clarity, where he stands before God and where he needs to be heading. Abraham increasingly realizes that he is but one small part in God's greater plan. His sentiments are similar to Ruth's. "The Kingdom plan is so much bigger," he says. "I must rely on Him more and wait for His leading. His will be done."

基督教

Since the church has gone "7-Eleven," Abraham says that his appreciation for team leadership has grown. That's because with this structure, in spite of the falling away of many members as a result of the shutdown, the church has begun to grow in numbers again. New people are coming to the meetings and are committing themselves to Christ. This time, though, the increase did not come about because of one large, impressive, flashy service. Rather it is the fruit of the smaller, multiple gatherings around the city that are being led by different co-workers. Abraham, in fact, has not been leading any of these groups. His focus has switched, for the moment, from shepherding the flock as a whole to nurturing and pastoring the leaders of these small groups. Today it is the small-group leaders who are carrying the bulk of responsibility for directly leading new believers to Christ, teaching them and ministering to their individual needs.

Abraham also says that the miracles and signs and wonders are continuing—again because of the faithful ministry of these small-group leaders and their members. He shares an episode from earlier in the year, when a small team consisting of different members from the various cell groups came together to accompany him on a visit to one of their church's missionaries.

This missionary is based in Yunnan province, and he had been sent to the southwestern part of the country to plant a church among a small minority group. Compared to cutting-edge Shanghai, this region is extremely backward, impoverished and even primitive. Many of the people there live in shoddy shacks that consist of one room, with dirt floors and no running water. As such, the living conditions are not easy. The plan for the three-day trip was to assist their missionary with his ministry in the daytime, including visitation to the villagers, and then hold evangelistic meetings in the evening. Upon arrival, and in preparation for the evangelistic meetings, the makeshift team from Wanbang decided to fast and pray when they sensed the place had a rather dark and heavy spiritual atmosphere about it.

During the course of their trip, their missionary introduced Abraham and the team to a middle-aged woman from the area. This woman, Mrs. Yung, shared with the Christians that when she was 19 years old, she had been raped. Because of this, her parents were ashamed of their daughter and kicked her out of the house. She was alone, had little education and was forced to fend for herself. Compared with other provinces in China, Yunnan is relatively undeveloped, particularly in the more remote areas inhabited by the minority peoples, and jobs are hard to find even if one is very qualified. Mrs. Yung was not; she was the epitome of inexperience. Hungry, cold and desperate, she ended up marrying a man who turned out to be cruel and forced her into prostitution. She suffered this husband for ten years, until at last she was able to get a divorce.

In the late 1990s, Mrs. Yung married her present husband. With him, she gave birth to a child. According to her husband, she was "one woman in the daytime and another woman at night." More specifically, she was like a demon at night—violent and with the foulest language coming out of her mouth. It was horrifying to see and hear her in this state.

Abraham and the team first led Mrs. Yung to accept the saving grace of Jesus Christ and confess His Lordship in her life. Then they prayed for her. As they did, they had a distinct impression that she was extremely unforgiving. It was so deeply rooted in her that it was as if a dark power was keeping her bound. The team asked Mrs. Yung if there was anyone that she had not forgiven in her life. She was forthright and named her parents, particularly her mother. So the team encouraged her to repent of this and prayed for her again. They sensed a breakthrough in her, as if she had been set free from this.

But when they looked at Mrs. Yung, again they noticed that there was still something strange in her eyes. As they pressed on in prayer for wisdom and knowledge of this situation, they discerned there was yet another source of bitterness within her. So the team asked her if there was someone else she had not forgiven. It emerged that Mrs. Yung was resentful of Mr. Yung, her current husband. She confessed that she had not married him because of love. She had married him because she felt she had no choice. As a result, she hated him, and in her dreams at night she pointedly cursed him. At this point, the team decided they should pray overnight before continuing their ministry to this woman.

The next evening, during the ministry time of the evangelistic meeting, they prayed for Mrs. Yung again. As they laid hands on her, she began to swear and curse vilely, and the team got a very good idea of what the night usually brought out of her. The voice and the language were clearly not her own. Abraham and the team allowed her to go on ranting in this manner for about 20 minutes. Then Abraham felt something rise up inside him and he commanded the demon to leave. "You have had a field day with her," he said with authority. "Now this woman belongs to Jesus. Her life can only have one master, and that is Jesus. Go! Leave her now!"

Abraham says he saw something physically depart from the woman, and he could tell immediately from her eyes, her face and the rest of her body language that she had been completely set free. "Her eyes became bright," he recalled, "and we could see that joy had literally filled her. All the bitterness was gone, all the hatred." Her husband could see the difference too and, as a result, he committed his life to the Lord.

By the end of the three days, more than 120 people had attended the evangelistic services, with a couple dozen accepting Jesus Christ as their Lord and Savior. They were also baptized in water and gladly joined the church.

In another miraculous story, Abraham tells the testimony of Miss Zhang. Miss Zhang lives in Shanghai and is in her mid-twenties. When she first came to the church, she was suffering from a disease called AS, or ankylosing spondylitis, which is a form of inflammatory arthritis. AS mainly affects the spine, though it can involve other joints, and it is chronically painful. In some extreme cases the inflammation can lead to a fusing of the vertebrae. In Miss Zhang's case her spine was visibly deformed, causing her to be permanently hunched or bent forward, and something as basic as walking up the stairs proved to be an agonizing task for her. Yet, this woman had become a believer in Jesus Christ and asked the church to baptize her by full immersion. Upon coming up out of the water, her small-group leaders and their team started ministering to her in prayer, asking for healing for her AS. During the course of their praying, the Holy Spirit revealed to them that this woman had deep-seated paranoia. She was intensely suspicious of people and accused them easily without provocation or reason. With this revelation the team decided to take some time to pray further about her situation. Ultimately, they decided to devote a period of time to fasting and prayer for her.

About a week later, they went to Miss Zhang's home to resume their ministry to her. Miss Zhang was lying in her bed as the team prayed for her healing. When they finished, the team noticed that she seemed very relaxed and that the bedroom was very peaceful. They left her home and allowed Miss Zhang to sleep for the rest of the afternoon. When she woke up in the early evening, she noticed that the chronic pain was gone. She did not feel the usual discomfort. Was it really so? She then decided to get up out of bed. To her absolute amazement, she was able to stand up straight! The curvature in her spine was gone. She was healed!

Miss Zhang went to see her doctor at the hospital. The doctor had compiled a long record of her AS over the years. Upon examination, the doctor and his medical team discovered that the calcification of her joints had ceased. In fact, her vertebrae looked normal now, restored to perfect health.

The healing from AS has only increased the desire in Miss Zhang to know Jesus. Today she is studying the Word of God faithfully and praying fervently. She also aspires to be a small-group leader in her church.

"More healings and deliverances like these are being experienced or brought about by the faith, fasting and prayer of the 'ordinary' members in our church," says Abraham. "It used to be that people would only go to the most senior leaders or the pastors on the stage to ask for prayer. But since the church was banned and we don't have that stage anymore, more grassroots people are stepping up in their faith. They are stepping out to do things like pray for healing for the sick or for those with broken relationships. It's something they never used to do before."

This is where Wanbang church is at today, and it's been an invigoration for Abraham's own faith. Throughout its decade of existence, Abraham has observed that the church has been through various phases. "When we first began, my main goal was to win souls for Christ," he says. "We were in a *kairos* window then, and we didn't have to do much. It wasn't us going out to fish. It was the fish jumping into our boat. It was so easy to win new souls for the Kingdom in those days.

"As we started to grow and became more of a formal congregation," he continues, "I decided to adopt some of the Korean methods of church building. We began to emphasize prayer in our church, and praise and worship music; and these became the main focus of my pastoral activities. But since being shut down by the authorities, our emphasis has switched again. Now we are working to train the believers to be close and intimate followers of Jesus, because some people couldn't take the pressure when we were banned, and they left the church. Some of them even left the faith." It is a sobering memory for Abraham.

"So now we are emphasizing the importance of going deeper into the Word of God, and the result has been quite encouraging so far. I see more leadership potential being developed since the shutdown, and for that I give glory to God."

基督教

Paul agrees with Abraham that the majority of unregistered churches are run in the family style. "There tends to be only one person who makes all the major decisions," he says. "If the life of this leader, or the impact of Christ in the life of this leader, is good, then that's fine. It's good for the church. But if there is little of Christ in the leader's life, there can be problems. So a team approach is always healthier and safer for the church. Besides," he says, echoing Benjamin, "one person cannot always be on a spiritual high. He will go through periods of lows. That's just life."

Expanding on the challenges confronting church leadership in China, Paul notes that society is changing all the time. This presents another dilemma: How well is the leader adapting to those changes? How well is he or she growing in his or her own personal life? Does he or she have the needed support to sustain real growth on a continual basis? "If he is the sole decision maker, it's not impossible to grow," he says, "but over a longer period of time, it's a lot harder to maintain. And what about God? Is the leader able to keep up with Him too? There are many leaders who keep to old habits and like the way things used to be—I know I do. It's hard for people to change. But sometimes we need to."

Paul cites Pastor Lin Xiangao from Guangzhou as an example. More commonly known in the West as Samuel Lamb, Pastor Lin was imprisoned in a labor camp for 20 years for his faith and his refusal to register his church with the government. Upon his release in 1978, Pastor Lin resumed leading Damazhan Church, which Rev. Billy Graham famously visited in 1988. Today, Pastor Lin is 88 years of age and continues to be the church's pastor. While greatly respecting and honoring the elder pastor for his perseverance and faith, Paul asks, "How sensitive will his decisions be to the needs of today's society? How well does he understand the post-1980 or post-1990 generations?"

For himself, Paul says that he is determined to step down from pastoring the church by the time he is 60. As the founder of his church, Paul could justifiably continue on as the sole leader, but he has chosen to pass on the baton well ahead of his retirement. He has already delegated authority among his leadership team, including the day-to-day management of the different meeting points and the setting and managing of the budget. His role has now been transformed into that of mentor to the district pastors, not unlike Abraham with his "7-Eleven" model, and they in turn mentor the cell group leaders. As the senior mentor, he periodically reviews church financial reports and advises on issues that arise, making suggestions on an as-needed basis. But his main focus today is Bible teaching and activating the missions vision of the church.

"I pray that the next generation of leaders for our church will rise up to the fullness of the calling God has on them," he says. "I pray that they will be sensitive to the Holy Spirit and understand what's needed for today's society."

基督教

"We need more leaders and pastors to have a Kingdom mindset." Abraham is talking about an area of bolstering that he believes is needed in the Church in China today. "We are not at unity," he continues. "More of us should be working together. But too often we are selfish, and we care only for our own assembly or what we personally think is important."

So what needs to change before the mindset improves?

"Everything begins with the heart of the leader, or the pastor," says Abraham. "Everything begins with what's inside." A leader can be gifted, he goes on to explain, and implement lots of systems, and have good organization, but these are only tools or methods. "Tools and methods should not be the deciding factors in a church. If the leader has issues inside his heart that haven't been resolved, personal or not, the tools alone aren't going to help the church mature or be sufficient for making decisions. And what will happen when the storms come?" he asks. "Will he have the character to do the right thing? Will he have integrity? At the end of the day, the type of leader one is will determine the type of church it is. The fruit the leader grows is the fruit the church will grow. The change needs to be made inside."

Another issue that he believes needs to be addressed in the Church, and that has arisen as a result of the modernization of the country, is that many of the younger Chinese Christians do not understand the purpose of the local assembly. They often view it as a social club. Consequently, "many people feel they can switch to a different church any time they feel like it," he says, "So they'll switch because they want to hear a better sermon, to be in a more comfortable place or because they prefer choir A to choir B.

"This understanding of Christianity is immature," says Abraham. "It's selfish and without real commitment. These kinds of people are on the lookout for what a church can do for them—whatever will satisfy their needs, whatever they feel like on that day. They do not consider that they might have a role to play in the church themselves. Sadly, it's a very typical attitude among the newer generation of believers. But this is not why the Church exists."

Paul puts it another way. He senses that "the urban churches are taking on more and more characteristics of a middle-class congregation, similar to that seen in Hong Kong, Taipei and Singapore. People are now fairly comfortable with their lives and enjoy modern conveniences and lifestyles." With food, shelter and clothing taken care of, he explains, there is nothing materially that they are really desperate for in their lives, hence the inclination to try different churches as if they were trends and fads.

The difference between the congregants in the Mainland and their Southeast Asian counterparts, he says, is that in the latter, "the believers tend to be second-, third- or fourth-generation Christians, and it is almost a tradition for them to stay very close to their churches. It is not unusual for the [Southeast Asian Christians] to seek counsel and advice about life decisions from the church. The believers in the Mainland, however, would not come to the church unless they were facing a crisis that was outside of their ability to resolve."

Historically, society in the PRC has been forced into submission, at times with brutality—the Cultural Revolution a case in point. The result is that the modern Chinese person can tend to be cynical about leadership and hold very minimal respect for authority. And now that the restraints have been cast off and there is more choice, they generally feel less obligated to be submissive or committed to anything or anyone.

To further emphasize his point, Abraham shares his observations on the effect the 9/11 attacks in the United States generally had on churches. "After it happened," he says, "a lot of people went to church. The same thing happened after the financial crisis a few years ago. People went to look for God, but it was only for a short while both times. It was like a fad. Again, the understanding and expectation of Christianity is that it is there to do what the individual wants at the moment."

His conviction is that if pastors and leaders truly want to see revival, they have to be willing to look beyond themselves. He says, "They need to be willing to live in a situation that is worse than the current one they're in, even if it means suffering. If there is no willingness to suffer, there will be no change or progress made in their ministries and, more importantly, in their own hearts and lives."

Paul quotes his namesake in the Bible: "For our light and momentary troubles are achieving for us an eternal glory that far outweighs them all" (2 Corinthians 4:17, *NIV*). "Through fire and water many Christians have been purified over the years in China. We need to keep pressing on."

"It's like the golden lampstand," says Abraham, referring to the lantern in the book of Revelation. "The church can only become the golden lampstand if she has the desire, the vision and the heart. Otherwise she will have no impact on the community for Christ when she goes out."

"And remember," says Paul again, "the lampstand in the Bible was beaten and hammered into the shape it was supposed to be. It was molded by the craftsman. God is our craftsman, and the beating and hammering is the persecution. Through our trials we learn to be obedient to the Lord. This is not an easy lesson. But how we fare in those times is the testimony of the Church to the world, and the testimony is what influences and leads to the glorification of God."

A self-proclaimed student of China's church history, Paul continues, "All those years that the Christians were holding secret meetings in their homes because of the threat of persecution—it was like the Church was a seed that had died and was buried. No one knew it was there because it was hidden. But then one day it sprouted. Everyone can now see the tree and its fruit, and now many more seeds have been produced for new plantings.

"We have to plant these new seeds," he states firmly. "We have to keep working the fields. God is giving us new opportunities in this new era, and we must be faithful to follow them up. We must continue to preach and teach the Word, and we must continue to help build up our communities. For our church in Xiamen, it means that we need to begin building when a new door opens for us. And we have begun. We commissioned eight missionaries to serve in Sichuan province in the aftermath of the earthquake, for the next few years. This is a new type of opportunity that never used to exist for us. We may not always feel adequate to be a sending church, but we have to start somewhere."

Abraham adds, "For the longest time, China has been on the receiving end of missions. It has been the one that has been served. Now we're at the stage where China needs to give back and pass on what it has received. In a perfect world you want to send the best and most mature people, but if we wait for that to happen we'll never get moving. We're human. We'll never be perfect. But part of the maturing process will come when we start to move. So we've got to move and take up the opportunities that come our way."

How can people outside China best pray for the Church in China going forward?

"First, don't pray for our problems to be solved quickly," says Abraham, "or that we will be persecuted less. Rather, pray that the Church will quickly learn the lessons God has for us and that we will mature. We *need* to mature. Second, pray that the pastors and leaders will be made more pure in holiness and that our intimacy with God will grow. Everything we do flows out of what is inside our hearts, so this is crucial for any ministry or service to God. Finally, pray that the church and the hearts of the believers will be purified. To God be the glory!"

Epilogue

"Watchman, how much longer until morning?
When will the night be over?"
The watchman replies, "Morning is coming, but night will soon
return. If you wish to ask again, then come back and ask."

ISAIAH 21:11-12

WHY WAS WANBANG CHURCH BANNED by the government? Why were Abraham and his team of leaders subjected to such intense pressure? Why does persecution still happen in China, especially when it has undergone so much modernization? These are some of the most frequently asked questions when people talk about what God is doing in China these days.

To begin with, Wanbang was singled out, among other urban churches, because it had become a "star" in the eyes of the officials. It experienced a tremendous growth spurt in a very short space of time, basically doubling in size every year for three consecutive years. But even more than this, it had connections overseas. A browse through their bookstore easily verified this, with translations and versions of popular American, Korean and Taiwanese Christian books available for sale, not to mention the fact that there was a mix of different nationalities in the congregation itself. Sizeable growth plus perceived cooperation (and therefore intervention) with foreigners raises security alarm bells as far as the authorities are concerned. That combination is an automatic strike against any church in China.

This then aggravates the second problem in the eyes of the authorities: Wanbang itself had strong leadership. It was obvious that the leaders of the church were influential—otherwise how could they obtain such growth? The leaders were gifted, charismatic people who were capable of motivating and mobilizing many people. When Chinese officials see this type of capability and attraction, it becomes a cause of concern for them. Will the Church prove to have more influence in society than the Party? Will the power of the officials be usurped? And so the authorities decide to apply *yali*, pressure, to suppress the rise of the church and to keep it under control.

But as Abraham says, why the persecution happens is not the important point. The most critical question is, *How will I respond?* Christians throughout the world need to give serious thought to this question. For the Church in China, the answer can literally be a matter of life and death.

The urban church leaders in this book are slowly maturing: They no longer consider persecution a curse, nor do they continue to believe that harassment and hardship should be automatically interpreted as demonic activity. In an ever-increasing way, they realize this is exactly what the Early Church went through. Yet, the Church has survived and even thrived in such difficult circumstances. The urban church is now more at peace about the whole issue of suffering. They understand that a certain amount of persecution is actually good for the church as a whole. It serves to make them stronger and more effective for the Lord.

Despite the ban, Wanbang Church was granted official permission to gather as a whole congregation for a special service on Easter 2011. Nearly 600 people crammed into a borrowed Three Self church building, with a capacity of only half that number, to celebrate their risen Savior. Meanwhile, in Beijing, Reuters[1] and BBC News[2] were reporting about how Shouwang Church members were being detained at their Easter meeting.

Why was pressure on Shouwang renewed? Undoubtedly there were a number of factors, but the primary cause was probably because Shouwang's actions and responses in the year prior were perceived by government officials as confrontational, particularly in the way human rights violations were cited and legal claims made to demand justice for their cause. This approach has led to some disintegration in the Shouwang leadership. Some leaders have subsequently left the church, believing that a more culturally sensitive approach should be employed in dealing with the government.

They now believe, as do Wanbang and other urban churches, that it is better to direct their efforts toward building relationships and trust with officials, to find common ground to bridge the gap. They believe that there are other ways to survive and thrive as a church. As of 2011, the leaders that remain at Shouwang are essentially trained or educated overseas and continue to favor more direct tactics for dealing with the Chinese government.

With respect to long-term cross-cultural missions, as far as the urban and rural house church leaders are concerned, how the believers respond to persecution at home is an indication of how well they will do in the field as missionaries. "We cannot use the Fuller School of World Mission principles to plant churches in Pakistan, Afghanistan and the Middle East," said Abraham, "or any other overseas model, such as South Korea's. The spiritual conditions in these regions are even more hostile than in China." Abraham explained that whenever there is persecution or suffering in China, such as what his church has been through, it is actually wonderful. "It's serving as part of the training or equipping for our next generation of workers for the mission field."

Not unlike what Robert Morrison faced when he first arrived in China, missionary activities in the places where the Chinese Church envisions going face a great many restrictions. Visas to stay are never guaranteed; neither are livelihoods or incomes to do so. And capital offences for what many in the West would consider infringements of basic human rights are very much in existence.

"These days," Abraham says, "the churches in the coastal regions, in the more prosperous cities, enjoy relatively more freedom, and officials are generally more open than in the rest of the country. But as you travel westward, the freedom to worship becomes increasingly restrictive."

Traditionally, it has been the case that east to west is the order in which policy changes are rolled out across the country—whether economic, social, political or, in this case, spiritual. Abraham went on to note that Tibet and Xinjiang province represent the farthest one can go west in the PRC. "You know," he pauses here to consider his words, "Wanbang was developed in a fairly open region of China. Now we've gone through some difficulty in preparation for the next region, which will be even harder. We've had to modify what we do; we're '7-Eleven' now, because it will gradually become tougher as we move farther and farther west."

基督教

Of what significance are the experiences of the urban church in China for Christians worldwide? Are there any practical lessons that believers outside the PRC can learn from the urban Church? If so, what?

We would argue that, yes, there are lessons to be learned. Global financial markets have seen chaos and turmoil in recent years with no clear signs of solid recovery in sight. Heinous acts of terrorism are no longer committed solely in traditional hot spots like the Middle East and Africa. The danger can literally be found anywhere today—Norway, Spain, the United Kingdom, the United States. The scale of natural disasters is incredible, with devastating loss of human life and destruction that is not relegated to "just" the Third World. News reports cover catastrophic earthquakes, tsunamis and volcanic eruptions whether they happen in Japan, Indonesia, Iceland or Guatemala. It seems that no matter where we are in the world today, life is uncertain, and there are troubles. Jesus said that such things will happen (see Matthew 24). But in the midst of the wars, famines and earthquakes, He says, don't panic. These things must take place.

Lesson 1: These Things Must Take Place

This is a hard truth to learn, especially for Christians who have grown up in relative prosperity and security. Most North Americans, for example, have not had to experience firsthand the atrocities of war or the desperation of famine and starvation. In truth, painful and costly sacrifices have rarely been required of us here. Think about the toughest spiritual choice you have had to make in recent times. When was the last time you faced persecution because of your faith? When was the last time you walked into your church service and wondered if this would be the day the government shuts down your assembly?

Nobody wants to suffer. Yet the biblical pattern in Acts reveals that the gospel was only carried and planted in other parts of the earth *after* persecution broke out. The oppression and pain that believers endured ultimately led to the wider distribution of the good news of Jesus Christ, and the further expansion of the Church.

This is the lesson Abraham and the rest of the urban church leaders are learning now. They are realizing more and more that they need to be willing to make the hard choices if they truly want to see God's will done in their churches, their cities, their country and in their individual lives.

The older generation of rural underground church leaders were forced into making hard decisions because of their circumstances. One spent weeks fasting and praying because, quite simply, there was no food in the land. One believed for the miracle of healing because there was no doctor or hospital for miles around. And one "preached" his or her testimony because that was the only thing he or she knew how to talk about. None of them went to Bible college. Most of them had not even finished junior high.

Most of the urban church leaders have not had to face such harsh choices. In comparison, their upbringing in the faith has been much more privileged. Their foundation to be effective church leaders is theoretically more ideal, with more education, knowledge, information, training and tools at their disposal.

The leaders interviewed for this book were asked as a group: What would happen if you were arrested, sent to prison and found that you had no more church to lead? Imagine that there were no cell phones, computers or any other way to stay in touch with other believers. After glancing around the room, at the ceiling and at each other, they answered that they would return to their "home village." Translated, this means that they would return to their spiritual roots—to the rural house church and its methods. They would pray and wait, like their country brothers and sisters, for the Holy Spirit to tell them what to do.

They were acknowledging, as Daniel did earlier, the intrinsic value of the rural house church DNA. In answering the question this way, they were basically admitting that in their hearts they realize this is indeed what they might have to face one day—that there may not be a church building left, that they might have to deal with a trial and imprisonment, that they may be abandoned and left sorely alone. Should that happen, it's time for the Holy Spirit to come to the forefront and shine. More than just realizing this, they accept it. If the Lord's will turns out to be different from what they had imagined, they will accept it, and they will change their course accordingly. It is not necessarily an easy thing to do, but they will change course, nonetheless.

Of course, Abraham has already gone through some of this, and it's been humbling for him. Yet, when he looks back, he acknowledges that in terms of the big picture, it has been good for him. His model for doing church has changed, he believes, for the better.

Ruth, too, has experienced a demolition lately—of her newly built business headquarters. The building, which also happened to house her new church premises, with a seating capacity of 500, was torn down because corrupt local officials incorrectly handled her project. The building was deemed an illegal structure and was removed. Her response to this crisis? "Maybe this loss of the building will bring me into a new level of relationship with my Lord Jesus. I prayed and sought His will before beginning, of course. I had my plan and my budget calculated, and I had worked out future projections too. But going to Jesus in prayer at that stage, I guess, was more like a formality. I wasn't desperate. So the biggest thing I learned from all this was that I still need to seek my Lord as a little child. I still need to trust Him and listen to Him." Ruth acknowledges that "it takes persecution, pressure and suffering to strengthen us in our walk with Jesus," and it is "through suffering that we are driven to the Lord."

One thing that becomes evident in talking with Ruth and Abraham is that neither one of them took their churches for granted. They never felt as though their plans or methods were the only ones that should be followed or that mattered. Sure, they had invested their time in prayer and in strategizing, organizing and drawing up their blueprints. But things turned out differently from what they expected, and some would even say disastrously. They had a lot and then they had nothing. Did this mean they were wrong or that their efforts had been wasted? No, because they know that in the end, His ways are higher than their ways and His thoughts higher than their thoughts, and they know that He is working for their good.

This is what it means when Christians pray, *Your Kingdom come; Your will be done.* It's submission to His lordship over their lives. Unfortunately, the word "submission" is very counterculture to the individualistic, self-centered societies many of us live in. With the focus always on "me"—*I* can have it *my* way; *I* can make this happen; the outcome is in *my* hands—where is the lordship of Christ in our lives?

Many Christians in wealthy and developed nations tend to have a sense of entitlement and forget that, in actuality, *it is the grace of God* that allows some to live and be born and raised in a place that already grants the freedom of assembly; the freedom of religion without fear of persecution; the right for Christians to express their faith; the right for Christians to claim tax deductions on charitable donations; and so much more. Many take these freedoms for granted. The challenge for believers is to ensure that Christ is, in reality, the King of our lives—in our actions as well as in our words. When He is on the throne, and we truly accept it, we will choose to stop demanding and pursuing our own way.

Another thing one notices when speaking with Ruth and Abraham—in fact with most Christians in China—is that no matter what kind of difficulty or persecution they are going through, or that has already occurred in their lives, they do not dwell on it. It is not the big thing or the focal point of their spiritual journey. Instead, Jesus is. Their habit is to view the hardship only in light of how much it brings them closer to their Lord and the lessons He wants them to learn. When in conversation with others, they are generally not inclined to be the first one to mention how they have suffered. They tend to talk about these kinds of things only if they are specifically asked about them. The reason for this is because they know that there are many Christians in the Mainland who undergo similar challenges in their faith. They are not the only ones.

But even beyond this fact, they can see that suffering was a part of the lives of Jesus' disciples. As Paul the apostle says, "you have been given not only the privilege of trusting in Christ but also the privilege of suffering for him" (Philippians 1:29). In other words, the Bible says that these kinds of things can happen. This is the way things were and the way things are. So they just get on with it.

If they are asked to give a testimony about a trial or difficult circumstance they have experienced, they will certainly speak, but usually with a deflection away from self, while attributing where they can the role that others also played in the resultant miracle, always acknowledging that it was "the grace of God." Hardship is just a part of life, they concede, a normal part of the faith experience. They know they do not live in a Hollywood movie; life goes on. It doesn't stop after a major battle or victory, nor does it necessarily end happily ever after.

Were there times when Ruth and Abraham couldn't fathom what was going on? Did they feel pressure, stress and frustration at having all their plans overturned? Did they ever feel angry or discouraged about their circumstances? Of course.

"These things must take place," Jesus said, and "the one who endures to the end will be saved." How will you respond?

Lesson 2: Go Back the Same Way You Came

Thirty years ago, the house church in China could simply be summed up as "Christ, the power of God." Miracles and healings were commonplace in the rural assemblies, and the church leaders portrayed a kind of daredevil approach to their ministries—they were always ready and willing to take giant leaps of faith. Today, however, the urban church is endeavoring to adopt a more balanced approach and is simultaneously moving toward "Christ, the knowledge of God," as the apostle Paul described in 1 Corinthians 1 and 2. Greater openness and "freedom" in China has meant that many urban Christian leaders (including those from the TSPM church) have taken the opportunity to visit well-known churches in South Korea, Singapore and throughout the West. Excited by the newness and the large scale of some of those meetings, they have brought back new ideas and have tried copying some of what they have seen abroad in their own churches. Yet, the leaders interviewed for this book acknowledge that some of the ideas they've picked up overseas have not necessarily been healthy for China's Church and have put it at risk of diluting the purity of faith established by the older generations of believers in the house church.

Trips abroad have spawned what some leaders are calling the A-B-C approach to building up the church—that is, placing an emphasis on Attendance, Buildings and Cash. The value of attendance is obvious: The thinking is that the larger a congregation, the higher the level of success attained. After all, isn't bigger supposed to be better, and the more the merrier? While in some cases there has, indeed, been an increase in the number of church attendees, it has not necessarily followed that there has been a growth in depth. In other words, the maturity or capacity to help the new converts develop in their faith is minimal. This could be problematic for the future Church, because it means that in some fellowships the roots are not growing deep or receiving enough nourishment. Without the depth, many of these new or younger believers will fall away when hardship and other difficulties arise.

In terms of buildings, the leaders in this book have discovered that the desire to build large-scale churches and a greater array of facilities, such as they've seen overseas, is superficial and has become an unnecessary burden to shoulder. In Beijing, for example, Shouwang Church is said to have spent 27 million *renminbi* (more than US$4 million) on a new building recently. In Hangzhou and Wuhan, other churches are reported to have purchased premises for 17 million *renminbi* and 10 million *renminbi* respectively (more than US$2 million and US$1.5 million). The prices of these properties are hefty in view of the fact that the average Chinese factory worker's salary is less than a tenth of the US factory worker's, according to the US Bureau of Labor Statistics.[3]

On top of the additional financial concerns, a church building in China brings with it a whole new set of challenges, unlike anywhere else. There is always the possibility that the church will become regarded as a political threat, not to mention the chance that a change in policy could lead to the meeting place being confiscated or even torn down at short (or no) notice. But beyond the potential political problems that come with a building, Daniel and several fellow pastors in Wenzhou concede that some of the larger venues in their city have become white elephants. A congregation of a few hundred people is dwarfed by their newly constructed 1,000-seat premise; in the case of Daniel's church, about 1,000 faithful regularly gather each week for worship in a venue that can accommodate more than 3,500. It is no longer a given that a new church building is a positive testimony, he says. "It can be something that is laughed at by officials and the local community."

How can Christian leaders ensure that their buildings and properties will always be used for the worship, celebration and glorification of God? How can they make certain that they remain places in which people can find healing, deliverance and salvation? How can they safeguard against their becoming mere monuments of things that used to be? These questions are also being asked, particularly by the branch of urban pastors who, not unlike Daniel, originally came from rural areas with the view to plant churches in the towns and cities. In their lifetimes they have seen the country shift from being an impoverished agrarian society to that of the affluent urban, and they have felt compelled to relocate and retool themselves in order to better fulfill their calling to serve the Lord and build His Church in the metro areas. But unlike their urban-born counterparts, who had the advantage of being raised in the cities, these rural-turned-urban pastors have had to travel farther to get up to speed in twenty-first-century China and have had to endure a steep learning curve in the process.

Less educated, generally speaking, a number of them discovered their knack for entrepreneurship by initially working in the small mountain factories that produced *shanzhai* or imitation brand products, such as cell phones, digital cameras and other electronic gadgets. After diligently saving their earnings, they then set up their own operations. Over the course of time these poor country pastors-cum-entrepreneurs—some of whom did not even wear their first pair of shoes until they were 15—began to see their businesses turn a profit. Shortly thereafter, property developers came knocking on their doors to ask if they could buy their shabby little factory buildings. How could they refuse the lucrative sums being offered? The deals also included new flats for the sellers of the properties in the proposed new developments. It was a win-win situation as far as they could see, and the pastors would find themselves with even more wealth than they had managed to accumulate while running their businesses.

The buildings were thus sold and torn down, and modern apartment blocks put up in their place. Yet these pastors did not desire to keep all of these blessings to themselves. They wanted to pass them on to their churches—after all, the main reason for their moving to the cities was to feed the Lord's sheep there. And in observing other urban church leaders around them, they noticed that some were purchasing properties and developing facilities for the benefit of their fellowships. It seemed a good idea to them, too, so they did likewise.

Yet, like the Wenzhou pastors, they have come to the realization that the blessing of a building can be very temporal. One can purchase a building with the best of intentions, and the presence of God can indeed be felt there for a while; but there can still come a time when He is no longer manifest in the place—and this possibility is frightening to them. The rural-turned-urban pastors had not anticipated this. If not the properties, what would there be of eternal value for them to pass on to the next generation of Christians in their fellowships?

As the great American evangelist Billy Graham famously said, "Our days are numbered. . . . The legacy we leave is not just in our possessions, but in the quality of our lives." Sometimes blinded by our zealousness, the temptation is to equate "legacy" with "monument," and we find ourselves endlessly striving to build or accumulate bigger and better things as a testament of our faith. Borrowing wisdom from another revered minister, Samuel Lamb, the elderly house church leader from Guangzhou who was incarcerated in the Chinese gulag for 20 years, says that eternal value is not found in tangible items. Rather, eternal value is found in the Word of God. Lamb, who is nearing 90 years of age, says that he has nothing to pass on to the next generation when he goes to heaven. The only thing he can do is to urge three principles on them. In an uncomplicated, plain manner, he simply says, "Preach the Word, in season and out of season. If you have a church, rightly divide the Word of God. Last, do all this even unto death." If his disciples learn or receive nothing else from him, he says, he hopes they will at least remember and put into action these three things.

In terms of cash, the urban leaders interviewed for this book have observed that in this day and age it does not seem to be a problem to raise money among the churches in China for the purpose of purchasing land or building facilities for a fellowship. Believers give freely and generously to those types of projects. In both Beijing and Hangzhou, for instance, as previously mentioned, churches have been able to acquire or construct new buildings in the past couple of years, as have Job's and Ruth's churches in Wuhan.

Yet, when it comes to supporting missionaries in the field or even workers in the church at home, there is much greater resistance to giving and allocating money for this. The salaries for those who serve in the Church continue to be substantially lower than other positions available in today's modern market. It is even less if one is not the head pastor, and the prospects are not particularly enticing for a young person considering whether to serve the Lord full time. How would one be able to survive in today's society? A young person from the rural area who chooses to move to a city to follow his calling to pastor or serve in a church can only expect to earn RMB1,000 (about US$160) a month. As is typical of many jobs for rural applicants, housing (usually in the form of a shared room) and food would also be provided as part of his employment benefits.

In comparison, the wages of an entry-level foot massage position could be four times higher (assuming the individual is willing to provide additional services beyond the official job description).

At present, the churches in China have no compunction about investing in buildings and facilities for their meetings, particularly since the cash is more forthcoming in the urban areas now. However, little or no investment is being made in the actual people of the church or, more specifically, in its future leaders. As one marketplace minister in the country observed, "From a business point of view, the Christians in China are more concerned with the building of bigger warehouses rather than developing better products or expanding their sales team. They put all of their money into their warehouses. They don't put it into their factories or their sales forces—areas that would strategically help the organization continue to grow and increase its profits. Their view tends to be short term as opposed to investing in or planning for the long term."

Some urban church leaders have imported an overemphasis on the importance of hierarchical organizational structure and "best practices" for their church. They have become more dogmatic in their beliefs, and the divine charisma—that is, the grace by the work and power of the Holy Spirit, which clearly used to characterize the house church—has become less apparent. In these places, the Church is under threat of becoming more ritualistic and less dynamic. Generally, these "new" and "improved" ideas have become extraneous trappings, at times being more imperative for the leaders to maintain than the actual Church herself.

Watchman Nee, the early twentieth-century Chinese Christian author who spent the last 20 years of his life imprisoned by the Communists, could arguably be credited with having established or set the house church model that has been and still is so instrumental in the Church's remarkable growth in the PRC. Born into a Methodist family, Nee was inspired by the Plymouth Brethren's belief in the equality of all believers. As a pastor, he modeled his church on the teaching that every day is the Lord's day, every home is the Lord's church, and every believer is the Lord's priest.

The "7-Eleven model" that Abraham now employs is exactly this, as it appears that the Korean and Western mega-church models are no longer officially tolerated. Instead of one large gathering, Wanbang Church is now comprised of smaller and more numerous meeting points spread throughout different neighborhoods of the city. As a result, church finances are better utilized today, primarily directed toward supporting workers in the field rather than keeping up the show, whether it was purchasing cutting-edge equipment for the stage or paying costly property rents and mortgages. As Abraham says, true worship is shown by how an individual lives his life each day, not by what he possesses.

How many white elephants do we have in the West? Have the maintenance and running of these oversized, cash-draining facilities overshadowed or become a higher priority than the actual care of the Church—the people?

If one considers the historical record of church planting and missions initiation in the book of Acts, one could argue that the overall development of the house church in China today more closely adheres to the pattern established in the Word than most of our church models in the West. The first eight chapters of Acts primarily focus on the stories of the men from Galilee, those who had little knowledge or education. The rural house church would arguably be the parallel here. Afterwards, up to chapter 13, the book chronicles the activities of laypeople, including those in the marketplace and those who were educated—not unlike the composition of the urban church in China today. This includes the adventures of Paul, Barnabas, Apollo and Silas—all of whom eventually became the learned elite of the Early Church. It was through the learned elite that the world ultimately saw the expression of missions to the ends of the earth.

Continuing with the pattern established in Acts, one could also contend that in the early years of the Chinese house church, prayer tended to constitute the initial bulk of activity, with meetings hidden or underground because of widespread persecution. The situation was similar in the upper room of Acts 1 and 2, where the disciples and others gathered, waiting for God to do something.

It was the despair and destitution that resulted from disastrous Maoist policies like the Great Leap Forward and the Cultural Revolution that originally drove believers in the rural house church to seek God. In those days the rural house church was solely focused on personal salvation. People were exhorted to call on the Lord for deliverance if they had problems, for healing if they were sick, and many saw and still see miraculous demonstrations of His love and power.

Through the years, this theological emphasis on evangelism in the rural house church has continued, and it is grounded in the Great Commission: to go and make disciples of all nations. But the custom of the rural church is to conduct their outreach primarily through one-on-one sharing, one individual or one family at a time. There is not the planned, deliberate strategy to holistically transform a whole community, like the urban church, by providing practical demonstrations of love through organizing social services or advocating social justice.

Gradually, the existence and growth of the house church became known to the wider public, and surprised officials, as the country slowly began to open up in the late 1970s and early 1980s. In fact, officials were astonished at the discovery of a vibrant and living faith, much like the religious leaders were of the Early Church in Acts 4:13, who "could see that they were ordinary men with no special training in the Scriptures." To their amazement, Christianity in China had not become obsolete or confined to the history section of the museum, as Mao's last wife Jiang Qing purportedly said.

The house church became an undeniable fact in the PRC, though it was never officially acknowledged—unless one considers the events of 2008. The Sichuan earthquake brought the unregistered house church, and in particular, the urban church, to the foreground. The government publicly recognized the Christians' unified efforts under the China ActionLove Volunteers Association banner in bringing relief to the victims of the natural disaster at a special banquet with President Hu Jintao. Consciously or not, the urban church took a major step toward distinguishing itself from the rural church. It was no longer hidden. It had come of age and was standing up with courage and boldness.

In the book of 1 Kings, we read that the prophet Elijah was hidden for three years before he called out the king of Israel and the prophets of Baal and Asherah on Mount Carmel. After a tremendous victory, where the Lord was revealed as God, Elijah fled in fear of his life because of the threats of Queen Jezebel. He went into hiding again, this time in a cave on a mountain. First Kings 19 relays how there was a windstorm, earthquake and fire on the mountain, but God was not in any of these. Instead, God was revealed in a whisper. All the noise and movement outside did not draw Elijah's attention; instead, it was a tiny whisper that caused him to cover his face in reverence and to emerge from the cave.

Throughout his life, Elijah was someone who had certainly seen God move powerfully in many situations—in truth, it was because of a tremendous feat by the Almighty that his life was in peril now and that he found himself in this cave!—but he didn't look for or rely on grand, flashy displays to know that He is God.

Too often, we think that we need to create a storm to get God's attention. We sing and shout our hearts out in our worship services. We strum our guitars and bang our drums at decibel levels that rival rock concerts. Perhaps we dance, clap and raise our hands. The intent here is not to disparage the worship of God through music; but it is clear that in some places today it has become routine and formulaic. Too many Christians in the Western Church come away from these meetings falsely believing that this is the only legitimate way to experience the presence of God. Jesus says, "go away by yourself, shut the door behind you, and pray to your Father in private" (Matthew 6:6).

The urban church leaders in this book are discerning that the ability to produce a slick, professionally run service has no correlation with the manifest presence of God in their meetings or in their individual lives. Rather, it's the opposite: It's the decision to take time each and every day to "be still, and know that I am God" (Psalm 46:10).

Samuel Lamb, the venerated senior pastor from Guangzhou, made the observation that many young church leaders these days are running around here and there, trying to do this and that, and generally trying to please too many. When someone is trying to please too many, he says, that is dangerous. This can lead to a loss of focus, which can then cause the leader to care more about making sure he or she fits in, is accepted and belongs. Self, in other words, becomes the real priority, as opposed to the people they have been called to serve, and this is actually insecurity on their part. "In truth," Pastor Lamb concluded, "when you have that assurance of belonging to Jesus, you will be able to stand in any situation. You *can* stand—even when you are alone."

The older generation of house church leaders, particularly those from the rural church, did not go into the cave of their own volition; they were driven there by necessity. They were trying to flee from the officials. Today, however, the urban church leaders are gaining appreciation for the benefits of spending time there, of being in the quiet. It is there, in private, to use Jesus' words, that they find the refreshing from God for their souls and the sustenance to see them through their trials and persecution. Hard times do not mean that they have somehow failed in their faith, or that they have sinned, and this is their punishment. They understand this now. In this sense, the urban church leaders are going back the same way they've come. They're returning to their Church's roots, which consist of valuing the rural house church's pillars of the Bible, prayer, evangelism, signs and wonders, and the willingness to sacrifice. These are the simple truths that helped them grow and mature in the faith in the first place.

Lesson 3: Let Your Yes Be Yes, and Your No Be No

Anything beyond this, Jesus says, comes from the evil one (see Matthew 5:37). That is to say, our words *do* matter. Yet, if we are honest with ourselves, many of us give little consideration to the meaning or impact of what we are saying. We tend to speak without a second thought, and the result is that in our liberal and free societies there are a lot of broken promises, unfulfilled commitments and an unnatural twisting of words that lead to disappointment and sometimes injury. This in turn can lead to cynicism, jadedness and a general lack of trust or belief in anything anyone else has to say. It's hardly an ideal environment for a Christian to share his or her testimony.

With most of the Chinese house church believers, there is something refreshingly honest and childlike in their approach to the faith. There is no artfulness in their speech; it is usually plain and straightforward. What you see is pretty much what you get. This transparent quality is not readily seen everywhere, nor is it always appreciated, and it is something that has been inherited from the older generation of believers in the house church. In my more than 45 years of ministry in the Mainland, it has never failed to impress me how these Christians not only value the Living Word and daily endeavor to put it into action, but also how guileless they are in doing so. They simply take the Lord at His word.

Over the years, some of the believers who have been arrested for their faith have been offered help (and what I used to believe was encouragement) in the form of letting them know that no efforts would be spared on their behalf, outside of the country, to raise awareness of their plight in the international media. By endeavoring to inform the world, the hope was that the authorities would be moved to exercise leniency. These believers were gracious and grateful for the offers, but ultimately they would say they only had one call they wanted me to make.

While reaching for my cell phone and wondering if a signal could be found in this place, my mind was bursting to know who the recipient of this all-important call would be. Would it be a government or a human rights organization? If there was anything that could be done, it would be!

To whom should I place the call? The answer, without fail was, "Call on the Lord." It was a stunning answer, completely unexpected and so humbling to hear. All our ingenuity, knowledge and network of contacts were not where these believers looked to find encouragement in their trying times, nor were they a means to extricate themselves from their situations. In the words of Paul the apostle, they were fixing their eyes "not on what is seen, but on what is unseen. For what is seen is temporary, but what is unseen is eternal" (2 Corinthians 4:18, *NIV*). In the end, they only wanted us to talk to God. The "help" they wanted was prayer—nothing more.

Corruption is pervasive in the PRC's pharmaceutical industry (as it is in other sectors), and the culture is such that it is considered a regular, normal mode of conducting business. When it became a known fact in her workplace that Job's wife had become a Christian, a colleague challenged her, questioning if it was right that she should still accept bribes and kickbacks. She could have laughed off her colleague's query and gone back to work as if nothing had been said. She could have justified such a response with, "It's just talk" or "Everyone does this. It's the way business gets done," and nonchalantly tried to blend in with the crowd. But she didn't.

With the heritage and reputation of the house church in the country, Chinese society, in general, not only knows of a Christian's integrity, but *expects* a higher standard of morals, ethics and behavior from the followers of Jesus Christ. Their interactions with believers over the years have shown them that words from a Christian's mouth can be counted on because they are almost always followed by a real-life demonstration of the person's professed belief. Words are not mere words; they are not communicated just for the sake of announcing something attractive or trying to make a sale, as in a propaganda or advertising campaign. Their words carry weight. They can be tried and tested. They will not be found wanting. They can be relied on as truth.

By merely stating that she had a newfound faith, Job's wife was now held to this standard. In Western societies, this may not seem like an issue of significant consequence. But many believers in the PRC know that there are ramifications connected to their choices, big or small, in everyday conduct. Ultimately, what they say and do will have a bearing on the strength (or weakness) of their testimony and on their influence in the world for God's glory. For Job's wife, this was indeed a dilemma. If she was no longer willing to conduct business according to accepted industry standards, then she would have to give up her job and substantial salary. There was a quantifiable cost to maintaining a good Christian testimony in her community. It was not a decision that she and her husband took lightly.

Would Jesus be pleased to see her continuing on with corrupt business practices? This was the critical question. She didn't want to just smile placidly and let her colleague's remark slip silently away. That would only send him the message that her words could not be counted on to carry truth; they were not worth consideration. She also didn't fall into the trap of allowing herself to be fooled into thinking that if she stayed at her job she would be there to share the gospel with others and help bring change to the industry. That all sounded good and reasonable on the surface, but deep down it wouldn't be the reason she stayed, and she knew it. She would be lying to herself.

She finally came to the conclusion that her actions must be consistent with her words; her whole life should be lived for Jesus and reflect His example, and this included what she did for a living, even if it meant finding a job that paid much less. She chose to resign and remove herself from the unnecessary temptations; she chose to honor the commitment she had made to follow her Lord and His ways.

At the same time, her husband also chose to change the emphasis of his surgical career to education. By choosing to teach and train more doctors, a greater number of people in China would benefit from his medical expertise and knowledge. In his role as a professor, he no longer faces the same type of pressure from the pharmaceutical companies to accept bribes in exchange for using their medicines.

Nonetheless, corruption is rife in the PRC, and it continues to muddy the waters for Christians who daily try to do the right thing in the marketplace. It is virtually impossible for a Chinese believer to completely avoid the graft. At some point, in one way or another, he or she will encounter it and face the predicament of either having to dole out bribes or gifts, or having to receive them. This culture of making payments to secure favorable treatment, goods or services is deeply ingrained and widespread in Chinese culture. It is not something that will be changed easily or in the near term.

So how do the urban church leaders deal with it? Some of the leaders in this book refuse to accept gifts or make payments, period. Others, in an effort not to offend the giver, and with a view to eventually leading the person to Christ, will "accept" a gift only on the condition that the giver understands it will in turn be donated to the benefit of a Christian ministry. Daniel and Job, for instance, have each, on different occasions, received gifts of costly Chinese artifacts from local officials who have been favorable toward them, but only after first informing the giver that the items would be sold and the money given to the church.

As far as Job and his wife are concerned, their commitment to Christ is as solemn a decision as when they spoke their marriage vows to each other. As such, their promises, declarations and vows are not disposable. They are not words that can easily be pushed aside and thrown away as soon as they no longer serve their purposes or are inconvenient.

The truth is that biblical values and principles are not always easy to adhere to. Sometimes they can be quite troublesome and leave you with what seems to be less, as Job and his wife have experienced. At other times they can also leave you standing terribly alone, like Abraham felt when his church was shut down by the government and he was no longer a "successful" pastor, with the largest urban congregation in the country. Elijah, too, stood alone. The prophet lamented in 1 Kings 19 that he was the "only one left" who was serving God. The masses had broken their covenant with God, he complained to the Lord, and were trying to kill him because he had not.

Today, wherever we live in the world, there are so many ways that we can communicate: We can choose to speak in words that are scriptural, diplomatic or politically correct. Alternatively, we can employ innovative methods to get our message across to others by using multiple platforms and new media, including social networking, all of which can be linked together with cute and clever marketing slogans. But consider this: Does our message, in whatever way, shape or form it is expressed, match up with our life actions? Do our "selling points" actually work, or have we fudged them in order to keep the package looking pretty? (This is an especially critical question if we are trying to share the gospel with the lost.)

If others buy into our message, will they find that what we say is true and trustworthy? Will they find that we keep the promises and assertions we make? Do our communications result in our ending up as another face lost in the crowd, or in our being a light that can be seen like a city on a hilltop? For someone who has been searching and journeying for a long time, the city on the hilltop is a sought-after and welcome sight. It means that rest and peace are near. The destination has been found. It's where they want to be.

Are our words disposable, or do we actually mean what we say? Are they the convictions of our heart and faith? Whatever we choose to express, and through whatever means or media, the Lord hears us. We will be held to account. That is why Jesus taught His disciples not to say anything beyond their yes or no.

Lesson 4: Wherever Your Treasure Is, There Your Heart Will Be Also

Jesus spoke these words in Matthew 6:21. What it all comes down to for each and every one of the urban church leaders in this book is that they believe deep down inside that they made the greatest discovery in life when they found Jesus. They're like the man who found a treasure hidden in a field and sold all that he had so that he could buy the field (see Matthew 13:44). They are sold out for Him, and their purpose in life has refocused to do their part to build His Church, no matter what it costs them.

For people like Paul and Job, the sacrifices have been costly. As the president of his air conditioning company, Paul earned more money in one month than in all the years combined that he has been a full-time pastor. Since Job became a full-time church worker, his income has shrunk to considerably less than half of what he earned by performing operations at the hospital.

Furthermore, Job's son struggled with shame and resentment against his parents when they decided to give up what Chinese society views as prestigious full-time medical careers to become pastors and missionaries. In the young teen's eyes, it was demeaning that his parents should no longer be doctors by profession, but church workers. Over time, though, and by God's grace, the family has been reconciled.

As individuals, their identity is in Christ, first and foremost, ahead of their profession, education or other qualifications. They say, "I am a Christian who happens to be a businessman" or "I am a Christian who happens to be a doctor." The rural-turned-urban pastors also think in like manner. When they saw that their society was changing, they did not bemoan the realization that they would need to make alterations to some of their methods in order to remain relevant. On the contrary, they were willing to be made uncomfortable, to be like a fish out of water for a while, until they became fluent in the language of modern China. Now, each of these pastors can say, "I am a Christian who happened to be born in a village, but I am willing to move out of my comfort zone if the Lord asks me to. I am willing to serve the needs of the people who live in the cities."

The urban church leaders in this book are always thinking about the Church. Picture a sports fanatic who studies the statistics of individual players and teams and is able to predict how they will match up against their opponents in the playoffs. The church leaders' desire to know the Scriptures is like the dedicated fan that knows a Major League Baseball pitcher's ERA or a fielder's batting average. Their desire to know their Lord and Savior more intimately is their passion, and they will make the effort and spend the best of their time and energy to do so. *How do I get closer to Him? How can I truly be holy? How can I help the Church grow into maturity? How can the Church guard against ungodly influences and stay pure? How can the Church shine brighter for God's glory?* These are the types of thoughts and questions that fill their minds. Their hunger for God remains deep.

The leaders also appreciate the fact that the Church is made up of many parts, just like the human body. Every part has a purpose and performs a different function; God has put each part just where He wants it, as Paul wrote in 1 Corinthians 12. Each part must come together and work together to move the whole body. Or, as Watchman Nee used to say, every believer is the Lord's priest.

They perceive that there are no superstars in the Church. As far as they understand from the Bible, the responsibility of sharing the gospel and making disciples of all nations rests with everyone who calls himself, or herself, Christian. This includes people in the marketplace, rural folk and city folk, rich and poor, old and young, children. The leaders each have their own church, but they regularly confer with each other, are friends with each other and proactively endeavor to find ways they can work together and help each other. In the process, they avoid getting distracted or drawn into divisive arguments over such issues as territorialism or protection of "my" church. They know that ultimately the Church belongs to Jesus Christ, and being able to cooperate with each other is healthy and good for the Kingdom.

Evangelizing, in the eyes of the urban church, is not just a one-on-one action, as their rural counterparts have so well done over the years. The urban church theology casts a wider net. As demonstrated by Job and Caleb, they are far more involved and assertive in matters of social development and concern. They are more missions-oriented, as seen by the ministries of Ruth and Daniel. They are also more organized and systematic in their training of the next generation of missionaries and leaders, as shown in the lives of Abraham and Paul. In fact, this group of leaders has even set up a school of missions in Thailand to train and equip missionaries, which China will one day send to the nations, in the not so distant future.

For these urban church leaders, it is imperative that those who are preparing for the mission field have a viable vocation or trade that will enable them to be self-supporting. The expectation is that the sending church will not continue to support them indefinitely. Some will argue that the rural house church has the same criteria for missionaries, but it is more difficult for those who are less educated, less qualified and with few practical trade skills to remain long term in a foreign mission field. Without the ability to be self-supporting, even issues like securing visas to remain in a country become harder to resolve.

The passion of the urban church has not gone unnoticed. Even a Three Self church pastor acknowledged off the record that there is a distinctive quality about the urban church leaders and their children. "Three Self church pastors don't have that kind of passion or nobility," he told me confidentially, "because our salaries and housing are guaranteed. There isn't the demand for sacrifice on our part like there is for them." In modern Chinese society, in the Communist mindset, to sacrifice is good and noble because it is all in service for the masses. In essence, they value the heart of the servant. This is one of the differences that people are noticing between the Three Self and urban churches.

Paul the apostle encourages believers to "have the same attitude that Christ Jesus had. Though he was God, he did not think of equality with God as something to cling to. Instead, he gave up his divine privileges; he took the humble position of a slave" (Philippians 2:5-7). Peter, meanwhile, teaches that God called us "to do good, even if it means suffering, just as Christ suffered for you. He is your example, and you must follow in his steps" (1 Peter 2:21). The desire of these urban church leaders is to follow Jesus all the way, even if it means suffering, because to know Him is the treasure in their hearts. What is your treasure?

基督教

When all is said and done, a greater degree of openness and more freedom in China are both a blessing and a challenge to the Church, as it also is elsewhere around the world. Opportunities to access and receive more Bible knowledge, Christian teaching and Christian resources are valued by all believers everywhere. At the same time, though, when the options seem endless, decisions can get more complicated and even overwhelming. Borrowing Abraham's analogy, how does one find the best from among all the Walmart deals? It is not always easy to discern what is good, what is right and what is not. All may be permissible, but not all is beneficial.

This is perhaps one of the most difficult challenges Christians face around the world today, particularly those who live in more affluent societies. You've probably heard the saying: he who dies with the most toys wins. Many people blithely laugh along with it. Yet, if one considers the actual meaning of those words, one would have to acknowledge that it is an aphorism that is not in line with the Bible; it is not a healthy concept, and we should not allow it to justify or have a bearing on how we live our lives before Christ. Choices are all around us, and they are not likely to get any easier given the constant development of innovative devices and a freer flow of information. Christians, if they want to overcome this glut, need to exercise more discernment and determine to be less lax and cavalier about entertaining unbiblical ideas.

The Church in China continues to face many challenges, as does the Church in other places. For most of the last 60 or so years in the PRC, it has generally been a nondenominational Church. But the state of non-denominationalism, as Samuel Lamb has keenly noted, was never "by our own doing. It wasn't by our own discipline. It wasn't by our own design. It was by the Communist Party. It was by Mao Zedong. It was by the closure of our country." Yet, the adoption of different kinds of theological emphases has been to the Church's detriment at times. Currently, the two largest influences in the country are the ultra-Calvinist and the ultra-Charismatic beliefs. Camps from both ends of the spectrum have formed and are creating conflicts and divisions within house churches, both rural and urban.

Pastor Lamb has seen the disagreements and factions, but he resists, in appearance and in actuality, taking sides. Over the years, he has received invitations to speak at numerous Christian conferences at home and abroad, but he has respectfully declined. "The conferences usually have a denominational emphasis," he explained. After a pause he added, "I don't need to go anywhere. I don't even want to leave my church. I have to take care of my church." Lamb further says that the state of having "no denominations does not automatically mean there is unity. Unity can only be possible when you have the Lordship of Jesus Christ above everything else. Walking in the truth and being guided by the Holy Spirit—that's where unity comes from. But the most important thing is to have the Lordship of Jesus first."

The nationalistic aim to catch up with the West has been an ongoing pursuit since the launch of the Open Door Policy. The generations raised since that time have all been driven by this goal. They have been totally saturated and immersed in this culture for the past three decades. Whether it's creating new technology, building the world's tallest skyscrapers or indulging in the consumption of luxury brands, the ultimate standard for the PRC has been the example of the West.

It has been no different for the Church. For the generations of church leaders that have grown up in the very same environment, educated by and following the same model, it can be a real battle to completely change an ingrained culture.

One of the areas the urban church leaders are contending with today is the dilution of purity of faith established by their forefathers—the older generation of house church leaders, of which Samuel Lamb is a part. With the Bible regarded as *the* manual of life, and one of the house church's five pillars, this automatic habit to "catch up with the West" has led to a major assault on their understanding of theology. The importing of questionable interpretations and stresses of the Word may not necessarily be falsehoods, but they are not the *whole* truth either. They are only half or partial truths, repackaged and marketed as "better truths."

These kinds of teachings have often been confusing and troublesome to the leadership in the Church in China because of the dubious fruit eventually produced in their fellowships. As such, they are dangerous for *any* church anywhere. Fundamentally, the gospel is "the power of God for the salvation of everyone who believes" (Romans 1:16, *NIV*). In other words, the purpose of the gospel is to save people. It is meant to transform human nature, not human standards of living. To suggest otherwise, while a nice sentiment, and at times well intentioned, is to diminish the power of Christ and His crucifixion. There is no "improvement" or better version of this truth available, no matter what anyone says.

"I would rather just see basic, foundational truth being taught," says Job, of the visiting Bible teachers to the Church in China, as opposed to some of the more elaborate doctrines that have come across his path. "Allow us to make our own theological discoveries. We are too young and not strong enough to defend against the dogmatic theories that are coming in. All these do is cause arguments and conflicts among the churches."

Ruth agrees with Job that some of the imported teachings have tended to bring more confusion than clarity. On the one hand, the exposure to different ideas has "brought us new insights and expanded our horizons," and she admits it's been helpful to "observe how things are being done in churches elsewhere." On the other hand, it has made what used to be straightforward theology obscure and unnecessarily complicated by assigning greater prominence to immaterial points.

Ruth believes that the Chinese Church does not need to aim so much to be sophisticated or advanced in its theology, training or organization. Submission to the Lordship of Jesus is vital, and in words somewhat reminiscent of Daniel's valuing of the house church pillars, she says that the Church needs to stick to the basics—stick to being faithful to read the Word; to memorize it; to put it into action, including reaching out and evangelizing the millions and millions of lost souls in the country; and to be faithful to pray and love one another. If those things can be done, she believes, the Church will be on a better track to the future.

There is no doubt that the battles come from within; but they also come from without. For the Church in China today, the toughest external battle is not against communism or atheism. The fiercest fight is against complacency brought on by the ever-growing wealth and ability to enjoy a lifestyle of comfort and ease. China became the second-largest economy in the world in 2010, when it overtook Japan, and the Organization for Economic Co-operation and Development (OECD) expects the country to over-take the United States by the end of 2016.[4] The PRC also boasted 95 citizens who earned places on "The World's Billionaires" list by *Forbes* in 2012—and this did not include 38 tycoons from Hong Kong who also made the tally. Overall, by country, China had one less billionaire than Russia, which came in second with 96. (The United States, of course, had the most billionaires with 425.)

For the average city dweller, the standard of living in the PRC has risen dramatically in recent years, and the increasing willing-ness to work overtime to be able to afford expensive brand-name products and conveniences is a strong motivation for many. Paul, the pastor from Xiamen, observes that "white collar work-ers are caught up in the rat race. They're worried about keeping up with their neighbors." Today the cost of living in the PRC's first-tier cities is comparable to that of places like Hong Kong and Singapore. Beijing and Shanghai, in fact, were recently found to be more expensive than the two Asian Tigers.[5]

This desire or compulsion to keep up with the proverbial Joneses has meant that some Chinese Christian urbanites have made nurturing their relationships with Jesus a lesser priority. They no longer have or want to spend very much time worshiping at church, praying or studying the Bible, and this has put pressure on some urban assemblies to change the way they do things. Paul explains that in times past, congregants were eager and willing to attend church services that would run literally all day, from morning to night. Today, however, with all the additional distrac-tions and diversions, some churches have felt the need to shorten their meetings to cater to changing lifestyles; many services in the cities now run for about one and a half or two hours, a duration not unlike that seen in churches in developed nations. The pastor from Xiamen has also noticed that in the cities there is now a considerably smaller appetite for all-day prayer meetings and Bible studies, which, at least for his church, used to be scheduled without a question of attending.

Ruth agrees with Paul. "The biggest opposition in our church today is materialism," she says without hesitation. "It's hard for people to overcome the temptation to keep buying and acquiring things." Consumerism is rampant in the country, Ruth says, and more people are enjoying the liberty and capability of "making money and spending money." This in turn has meant that they are now "taking life much easier," which leads to complacency. Her sense is that with most people life is fine; it has become comfortably routine and pleasantly predictable. They are content to keep it that way, too—but this is an attitude they need to guard against in the church.

"We still have a lot of ladies in our church and, therefore, the prayer life is still very active—for now at least," Ruth says. "But they are also struggling. It is growing more difficult for them to get their husbands involved at church, and their children. The husbands are always working and trying to make more money, and with the children, their studies take up so much of their time and attention."

Abraham says that in his church, too, they have felt the same kinds of pressure. "As a church," he says, "we are struggling with our prayer meetings." He is not talking about a monthly or weekly gathering. He is talking about a daily Monday to Sunday gathering at five o'clock in the morning to intercede for the church. "Our team will lead the people in these prayers every day. But we don't know how long this can be maintained."

When Wanbang Church first began a little more than 10 years ago, the members tended to be less sophisticated and have less financial means. In those days they were content to devote many hours to prayer and were more open to helping the church in different ways. Today, however, "the congregants, particularly the younger ones, have different lifestyles. They are more into shopping, vacationing, surfing the Internet, playing video games and acquiring the latest electronic gadgets." He says that Shanghai people are now no different from those in the busy metropolises of Hong Kong, New York or Tokyo. Their lifestyles are "very hectic, very busy and very driven."

Daniel concurs. "Materialism and consumerism are the greatest challenges in discipling the new believers in the cities. They need to see solid, good role models in their leadership—in the pastors, the elders and the deacons."

Daniel's comment leads to the other effect that growing wealth and prosperity have had on the urban churches: This is in the area of leadership. The higher incomes in the Christian fellowships have commonly been accompanied by more professionally qualified and more highly educated members—including lawyers, accountants, architects and doctors. Increasingly, these professionals have moved into positions of church leadership. This has led to a less than ideal situation in some churches whereby the premium value of leadership is no longer placed on the servant's heart for God, his calling and biblical foundation; rather it is placed on one's academic background or career achievements in the marketplace.

There are even instances where social standing in society is also revered. But, Job says, these professionals "were never taught leadership with Christian values. They are being recognized in the churches because of what they've achieved out in the world." Job says that when these (predominantly) first-generation believers exercise leadership in a church, they tend to do so with many conflicts of interest, which in turn create more problems for the fellowship.

"You have to remember the way we were raised," he explains. "Our whole way of thinking, our whole value system was based on revolutions, anti-revolutions and class struggles. Our greatest lack—and I include my church, our teams and myself here—is that we've had very little exposure, in comparison, to Christlike leadership, to Kingdom values or a godly mindset. None of this was ever in our blood or in our veins. So, while we are growing, we still have much to learn." The lack of godly leadership, to him, is the number one challenge confronting the urban house church in its ability to grow further and mature.

The leadership challenge is not just an issue for today. An insufficient investment into the next generation of leaders does not bode well for the future prospects of the Church in China. Why? For the simple reason that if there are no shepherds, the sheep will scatter.

In the first place, there is, unfortunately, a prevailing attitude among some of the more experienced and longstanding pastors that because there are not enough mature or qualified leaders, they must continue to shoulder the burden alone. These ministers do not view the situation as an opportunity to pull together the different parts of the Body of Christ, to build teams within their assemblies or to mentor future leaders. In this regard, they tend to lack long-term vision; and while paying lip service to the need, their efforts to develop the next generation of leaders continue, for the most part, to be virtually nonexistent or a low priority.

In the rare case where a church does avail training for young up-and-coming pastors and church workers, the modes employed have usually not been well thought out or involved any serious input of resources or time to find the necessary experts to teach. Sadly, in most cases, the leadership training on offer ends up consisting of a visit from an older pastor who usually preaches whatever message he happened to speak on the previous Sunday in his own church.

This turns out most often to be the case for the prospective leaders who originate from the rural areas. Their training options are considerably more limited in comparison with their urban counterparts because of their locale and, more significantly, because they are more likely to fall short in the educational requirements to qualify for a proper local (Three-Self) seminary. If they then want to apply for a course at a school outside of the country to secure their theological education, they face two more obstacles: First, they would need to qualify academically, which is unlikely if they were unable to do so at home; and second, they would in all likelihood lack the financial means to go. They face an acute situation: There are no proper Bible courses within their reach, from an accredited school, and with a comprehensive syllabus and materials available for deeper study.

On the other hand, as an increasing number of unregistered churches become more organized with better financial management and governance structures, including forming elder and deacon boards, there is a real danger that they will lose their vibrancy and dynamism. Some of the urban church leaders in this book even fear that they could become more like the Three Self churches. "We cannot fall into the trap of allowing the system to take over the work of the Holy Spirit," says Abraham.

Put another way, Ruth says that the problem with some of the ideas that some leaders are bringing into their churches today, from Christians outside of the country—including better organization and more orderliness—is that they tend to "emphasize methods and ways of doing things with our human ability." Ruth further says that these approaches can be rigid or restrictive, yet the Chinese Church has traditionally been quite flexible over the years and open to the movement of the Holy Spirit.

On the whole, the urban church in China continues to grow rapidly, and the rural-turned-urban leaders play a crucial role, bringing with them the riches of the rural church's heritage to add further fuel to the fire in the cities.

As stated at the beginning of this book, the urban Church's story is really only beginning. We have shared but a handful of the top leaders' stories. There are and will be many more leaders and stories to tell. These leaders you've read about are not celebrities. They are very much ordinary, white-collar professionals who go to work from 9 to 5 yet also manage to run a church at the same time.

Some are, of course, choosing to become full-time ministers, such as Paul and Job. Believers worldwide can be inspired and encouraged by their testimonies, especially those of us who live in the industrialized world. Here are people just like us: They've had trouble in their marriages and families; they've had failed businesses and personal financial struggles; they've faced moral dilemmas in their society, yet they are holding steadfast to their Lord and Savior. And it goes without saying that they live under constant scrutiny from officials, with the pressure crushing at times.

In Caleb's case, for example, he made the heart-wrenching decision to allow his son to be adopted for his own safety by a kindly pastor from Singapore. Threats to kidnap his 10-year-old boy have been made by triads who, in turn, were hired by some corrupt local officials in an effort to coerce Caleb into selling them a piece of land. Caleb and other pastors are coming through the fires, though, and they're being refined as gold. Or, as the ever-faithful Pastor Lamb from Guangzhou said to the police when they last came to visit him, "I'm all packed. I'm ready to go to prison."

If they can do it, why can't we?

The full impact of the urban Church in China on the global Church remains to be seen. For the time being, it will be minimal. But as Jesus said:

> God blesses those who are poor and realize their
>   need for him,
>   for the Kingdom of Heaven is theirs.
> God blesses those who mourn,
>   for they will be comforted.
> God blesses those who are humble,
>   for they will inherit the whole earth.
> God blesses those who hunger and thirst for justice,
>   for they will be satisfied.
> God blesses those who are merciful,
>   for they will be shown mercy.

God blesses those whose hearts are pure,
for they will see God.
God blesses those who work for peace,
for they will be called the children of God.
God blesses those who are persecuted for doing right,
for the Kingdom of Heaven is theirs
(Matthew 5:3-10).

As long as they continue to desire to be more like Christ and search for Him with all their hearts, they will be, as Ruth says, on the better track. Another point in their favor is the fact that their DNA is derived from the rural house church—founded in the Bible, prayer, evangelism, signs and wonders, and the willingness to pay a price. Therefore, their influence for good should continue to grow. Yet, they have still to develop their own indigenous church pattern and theology and compose their own worship songs and hymns. Until they are able to do these things, their substance will need further nurturing and maturing.

As Abraham asks, keep praying that the urban house churches in China will grow in their maturity and purity before the Lord so that their light can truly continue to shine, even to the end of the world. They're praying for you too.

Notes

1. Ben Blanchard and Chris Buckley, "Chinese Police Detain Christians as Dispute Spills into Easter," *Reuters* (April 24, 2011).
2. "China Detains Protestant Shouwang Devotees," *BBC News*, http://www.bbc.co.uk/news/world-asia-pacific-13180842 (April 24, 2011).
3. Bonnie Kavoussi, "Average Cost of a Factory Worker in the U.S., China and Germany," *Huffingtonpost.com* (March 8, 2012).
4. Josephine Moulds, "China's Economy to Overtake US in Next Four Years, Says OECD," *The Guardian* (November 9, 2012).
5. Te-Ping Chen, "Beijing, Shanghai Cost-of-Living Leaps," *The Wall Street Journal* (December 12, 2012).

Appendix

China Chronology

Date	China	Church in China
1949	Mao Zedong and the Communists come to power.	
1951-54	Suppression of counterrevolutionaries and Three- and Five-Anti campaigns.	Foreign missionaries expelled from China. Three Self Patriotic Movement church instituted by government, in which churches are to be self-governing, self-supporting and self-propagating. Three Self churches were initially opened in cities only.
1955-56	Communist attempt to purge hidden counterrevolutionaries and Hundred Flowers Bloom campaign.	Some pastors and other Christians are arrested and imprisoned.
1957-61	Anti-Rightist and Great Leap Forward campaigns.	Some pastors and other Christians arrested and imprisoned. Rural house churches begin to emerge, independent of the Three Self churches.
1966-76	Cultural Revolution. Mao Zedong dies (1976).	All churches officially shut down, including Three Self churches. Rural house churches continue to emerge. Some pastors and other Christians arrested and imprisoned.

1978-79	Deng Xiaoping becomes paramount leader. Open Door Policy launched including the establishment of special economic zones in Shenzhen, Xiamen and other cities.	Some pastors and other Christians exonerated and reinstated into society. Three Self churches are reopened. Rural house churches continue to flourish. Some urban house churches begin to meet, independent of the Three Self churches.
1983	Anti-Spiritual Pollution campaign.	Some pastors and other Christians arrested and imprisoned.
1989	Student demonstrations in Tiananmen Square (Beijing).	Rural house churches continue to flourish. The urban house church movement gains momentum.
1997	Deng Xiaoping dies. Jiang Zemin succeeds him.	The urban house churches begin to flourish and connect with churches outside of the country.
2002	Hu Jintao succeeds Jiang Zemin.	

About the Authors

REV. DR. DAVID WANG is Founder and General Director of Hosanna Foundation and President Emeritus of Asian Outreach. A Shanghai native, he has been based in Hong Kong since 1957, when he first came to the city as a child refugee. Today, after 47 years as a missionary, David is one of the foremost experts on the Church in the People's Republic of China and is a much sought-after speaker at international missions conferences. As an author, David's other books include *Still Red* and *The Coming Influence of China*. He has also published more than 20 titles in Chinese.

Hosanna Foundation was established in 2010 to steer the growth of the various China ministries of Asian Outreach with the view to eventually transferring their leadership and ownership to the Church in China herself. As such, Hosanna is "pastoring the pastors to pastor, training the trainers to train, and leading the leaders to lead in the Church of China." www.hosanna.org.hk

GEORGINA SAM was born and raised in Canada to Chinese immigrants. She currently lives in Hong Kong. In addition to *Christian China and the Light of the World*, Georgina is the coauthor of *Still Red* and *Generations*. Her writing has also been published online at the *Still Red Blog* and *AmiraCulture.com*.

To contact David and/or Georgina, email info@hosanna.org.hk.

Also Available from
Regal Books

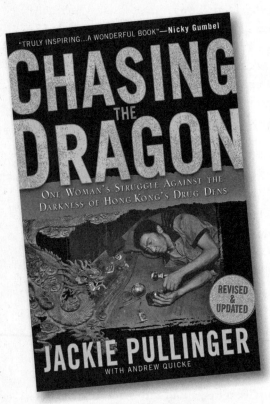

Chasing the Dragon
Jackie Pullinger
ISBN: 978.08307.43827

Inside of Hong Kong was the infamous Walled City. Strangers were not welcome there. Police hesitated to enter. It was a haven of filth, crime and sin. Prostitution, pornography and drug addiction flourished. Jackie Pullinger had grown up believing that if she put her trust in God, He would lead her. When she was 20 years old, God called her to the Walled City. She obeyed. And as she spoke of Jesus Christ, brutal hoods were converted, prostitutes retired from their trade and heroin junkies found new power that freed them from the bondage of drug addiction. Hundreds discovered new life in Christ. Chasing the Dragon tells the whole amazing story—exactly as it happened.

Prepare to be inspired by the testimony of a life given over to the poor and forgotten and the amazing blessings that resulted.

Available at Bookstores Everywhere!

Go to **www.regalbooks.com** to learn more about your favorite Regal books and authors. Visit us online today!

Regal
God's Word for Your World™
www.regalbooks.com